1000 FACTS ON
FOSSILS

First published in 2007 by Miles Kelly Publishing Ltd
Bardfield Centre, Great Bardfield, Essex, CM7 4SL

Copyright © 2007 Miles Kelly Publishing Ltd

2 4 6 8 10 9 7 5 3 1

Editorial Director Belinda Gallagher
Art Director Jo Brewer
Assistant Editor Lucy Dowling
Junior Designer Candice Bekir
Picture Researcher Laura Faulder
Production Manager Elizabeth Brunwin
Indexer Jane Parker
Reprographics Anthony Cambray, Ian Paulyn

British Library Cataloguing-in-Publication Data
A catalogue record for this book is available from the British Library

ISBN: 978-1-84236-899-2

Printed in China

www.mileskelly.net
info@mileskelly.net

1000 FACTS ON FOSSILS

Chris and Helen Pellant

Consultant: Steve Parker

Miles Kelly

PUBLISHING

Contents

WHAT ARE FOSSILS?

What are fossils?	8	Evolution	18
Fossils and time	10	Tracks, trails and burrows	20
Collecting fossils	12	Rocks made of fossils	22
Naming and caring for fossils	14	Microfossils	24
Extinction	16	The oldest fossils	26

FOSSIL PLANTS

Fossil algae	28	Glossopteris and	
Primitive plants	30	Continental drift	38
Fossil plants and coal	32	Ginkgo and other living fossils	40
Coal-forming plants	34	Mesozoic and Cenozoic plants	42
Mazon Creek, Illinois	36		

CORALS, SPONGES AND ECHINODERMS

Fossil corals	44	Brittle stars	60
Lower Palaeozoic corals	46	Jurassic sea urchins	62
Time recording in the Palaeozoic	48	Spiny sea urchins	64
Jurassic reefs	50	Burrowing sea urchins	66
Fossil sponges	52	Brachiopods	68
Fossil crinoids	54	Palaeozoic brachiopods	70
Encrinus and the Triassic		Rhynchonellids	72
of Germany	56	Terebratulids	74
Jurassic crinoids	58		

Contents

GRAPTOLITES AND ARTHROPODS

Graptolites	76	Silurian trilobites	90
Graptolites and geological time	78	Trilobite defence	92
Arthropods	80	Butterfly stones	94
Giant sea scorpions	82	Very small trilobites	96
Fossil insects	84	Trilobite vision	98
Fossil crabs	86	Continental drift and trilobites	100
Giant trilobites	88		

MOLLUSCS

Molluscs	102	Ammonites	126
Bivalve molluscs that swim	104	Ammonite variety and movement	128
Fossil oysters	106	Ammonite suture lines	130
Cenozoic bivalves	108	Spiny ammonites	132
Burrowing bivalves	110	Ammonite names	134
Freshwater bivalves	112	Giant ammonites	136
Fossil gastropods	114	Uncoiled ammonites	138
Cenozoic sea snails	116	Ammonites as zone fossils	140
Predatory sea snails	118	Cretaceous ammonites	142
Cephalopods	120	Ammonites with beaks	144
Devonian and Carboniferous cephalopods	122	Fossil squids	146
Modern and Jurassic nautilus	124	Tusk shells	148

VERTEBRATES

Vertebrate fossils	150	Early amphibians	160
Early fossil fish	152	Mosasaurus	162
Armoured fish	154	Pliosaurus and Plesiosaurus	164
The Green River fish	156	Ichthyosaurus	166
Fossil fish teeth	158		

DINOSAURS

Dinosaurs	168	Deinonychus	184
Stegosaurus	170	Pterodactyls	186
Triceratops	172	Diplodocus	188
Compsognathus	174	Footprints and dinosaur	
Allosaurus	176	movement	190
Iguanodon	178	Dinosaur eggs and nests	192
Saurolophus	180	Archaeopteryx	194
Tyrannosaurus	182		

MAMMALS

The first mammals	196	Giant whales	202
Megatherium	198	Ice Age monsters	204
Paraceratherium	200	Hominid fossils	206
Glossary	208	Index	210

What are fossils?

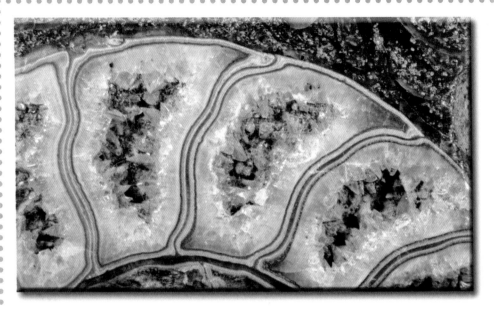

▲ *The internal chambers of this ammonite shell have filled with crystals of calcite during fossilization.*

- **Fossils** are the remains of, or evidence for, past life preserved in the rocks of the Earth's crust.

- **For the remains** of an organism to be preserved, it has to be made of material that is stable in the sediment (mud and sand) in which it is buried.

- **Usually shells**, bones, plant stems and other remains are changed into minerals, such as calcite and quartz, for them to be preserved.

- **Creatures and plants** with hard parts are more easily preserved, as they are not easily broken before they are buried in sediment.

8

- **Some fossils** are simply the impressions of a shell or other organism on a rock surface. All the solid parts of the creature have disappeared.

- **Most fossils** are of organisms that lived in the sea, because here most sediment is deposited.

- **Sometimes**, whole organisms are preserved almost unaltered, such as insects trapped in amber, or mammals preserved in frozen ground.

- **Only the tiniest** fraction of creatures and plants that have lived are preserved in the 'fossil record'.

- **Scientists** who study fossils are called palaeontologists and the science is called palaeontology.

▶ *This delicate insect has been preserved complete, encased in amber.*

...FASCINATING FACT...
Some of the most delicate organic remains that have been fossilized include the feathers of primitive birds, the wings of dragonflies and the leaves of plants.

Fossils and time

- **Palaeontologists** are able to use fossils to work out many details about the Earth in the past, including how old strata (rock layers) are.

- **The sediments** in which fossils are preserved were deposited in layers, with the older layers below younger ones.

- **Certain strata** are characterized by particular fossils, and these rocks can be correlated from place to place by using their fossils.

- **Fossils** that are widespread geographically are best for this linking of strata from one area to another.

- **Fossils from the Jurassic Period** found in Britain, Europe, the Himalayas and South America tell us that rocks in these now distant regions formed at exactly the same time.

- **Fossilized species** that only existed for a short time will only be found in a relatively thin layer of rock, and so will allow accurate correlation.

- **Ammonites and graptolites** are excellent for the relative dating of rocks.

◄ *This large ammonite, fossilized in limestone, has been eroded to reveal the suture lines.*

- **The relative geological time scale** has been established by using fossils and other geological principles.

- **Radiometric dating** is used to give absolute dates to the various parts of the time scale.

- **The time represented** by a given fossil species is called a zone, and may be as brief as 750,000 years.

▼ *This time chart shows how geological time has been divided by geologists. The absolute dates (the numbers) have been worked out using radiometric dating methods.*

ERA	PERIOD	EPOCH	AGE (MYA)
CENOZOIC	Neogene	Holocene (Recent)	From 0.01
			1.8–0.01
		Pleistocene	5.3–1.8
		Pliocene	23–5.3
		Miocene	
	Palaeogene	Oligocene	34–23
		Eocene	56–34
		Palaeocene	65–56
MESOZOIC	Cretaceous		142–65
	Jurassic		206–142
	Triassic		248–206
PALAEOZOIC	Permian		290–248
	Carboniferous		354–290
	Devonian		417–354
	Silurian		443–417
	Ordovician		495–443
	Cambrian		545–495
PRE–CAMBRIAN TIME			4500–545

11

Collecting fossils

- **Some of the most famous** and important fossils have been found by chance, but it is wise to make plans before you go collecting.

- **Fossils occur** mainly in sedimentary rocks, so there is no point looking in areas where granite or other igneous rocks occur.

- **Sedimentary rocks** such as limestone, mudstone, sandstone and shale are formed in layers, usually on the seabed.

- **Road cuttings**, stream valleys and sea shores are good places to look for fossils, as here strata are exposed and can be easily seen.

- **A geological map** is useful to find out where sedimentary rocks, which may contain fossils, occur, but a map may not show exactly where the rocks are exposed. Strata are often obscured by buildings and roads, soil, plants and trees, and glacial debris.

- **Rocky coasts** are very good places to find fossils, as here rocks are constantly being eroded. Cliff falls bring fossil-bearing rock down to beach level. However, they should be approached with caution. Many geologists have been injured, and some killed, by rock falls from cliffs.

- **Permission** must always be sought before going onto private land, and you should never go alone.

- **A geological hammer** is useful for breaking up rocks containing fossils. Do not use an ordinary woodwork hammer, as the metal it is made of is very soft.

- **There is often no need** to quarry away at strata. Fossils are readily obtained from fallen and eroded rocks.

- **All fossils** are of scientific importance. Always wrap any specimens carefully, and record in a notebook where and when you found them.

12

▲ *Fossils have to be carefully removed. Here, dinosaur bones are encased in plaster before they are carried away.*

Naming and caring for fossils

- **Fossils are biological material**, and they are named according to the principles of biology.

- **This system**, still used today, was established in the 18th century by Carolus Linnaeus, a Swedish naturalist. Because there was a different name for each plant and animal in each language, he used mainly Latin names.

- **An organism** is generally given two names. The first is its generic name and the second its specific name.

- **The ammonite** *Hildoceras bifrons* belongs to the genus *Hildoceras*. This contains a number of species, of which *bifrons* is one. Note that biological names are written in italics.

- **These Latin words** have significance and meaning. *Hildoceras*, for example, is named after St Hilda, whose Abbey is at Whitby in North Yorkshire. This ammonite is common in strata there. The species name '*bifrons*' describes the two 'brows' or ridges running around the edge of the fossil.

- **To name fossils** that you have found, it will usually be necessary to compare them with those shown in one of the many illustrated palaeontology books or Internet sites.

- **Expert help** will be available at a local museum or university if you are unable to work out the name for a certain fossil.

- **Your fossils** will have to be cleaned, and any excess rock or dirt carefully removed.

◀ *These fossil molluscs have been placed in card trays, with labels to stop them rubbing against one another.*

● **It is best** to keep each fossil in a small card tray, so that there is no chance of them rubbing together.

● **The details of each fossil**, taken from your notebook, can be written on a card beneath the specimen. A number of these trays can be kept in a single drawer.

15

Extinction

- **When a species dies out**, for whatever reason, it is said to be extinct. Similar species may continue to survive, but that unique species has gone forever.

- **The fossil record** contains many breaks. A series of fossils that can be traced from layer to layer may suddenly come to an end, showing that those creatures became extinct.

- **Extinction** of one group of organisms can allow another to develop and flourish, so extinction allows the evolution of other species to take place.

- **There are countless** examples of extinction to be found when fossils are studied, from the dinosaurs to small molluscs.

- **The causes of extinction** are varied, but environmental changes can cause the death of many unrelated species, as may have happened at the end of the Permian Period, 248 million years ago.

- **A classic case** of extinction, which has been studied in detail, is that of the dinosaurs at the end of the Cretaceous Period, 65 million years ago.

- **There is considerable evidence** for a widespread change in climate and sea levels at the end of the Cretaceous Period.

- **Evidence** from various places shows that a large meteorite may have hit the Earth at about this time.

● **Dust from this meteorite impact** would obscure the sunlight and kill plants. Food chains would then be destroyed, causing widespread extinction of many different animals.

...FASCINATING FACT...
When the dinosaurs became extinct, so did 75 percent of marine plankton, and very successful creatures such as the marine ammonites.

◄ *Ammonite fossils. Ammonites became extinct at the end of the Cretaceous Period, 65 million years ago.*

Evolution

- **Evidence** for the development of life into its various forms can be found in the record of fossils. This change from one living thing to another is called evolution.

- **By looking at fossils**, it can clearly be seen that the more primitive plants and animals are found in the oldest rocks. However, the trilobites, which occured as long ago as the Cambrian Period (545–495 million years ago), were very well-developed creatures.

- **Evolution** is not always a steady process. It has many sudden jumps when organisms develop rapidly.

▼ *Trilobites appeared at the beginning of the Cambrian Period. They probably evolved from soft-bodied pre-Cambrian creatures.*

- **During the Pre-Cambrian Era** (before 545 million years ago) life was probably very primitive, but for various reasons the fossil record from this time is extremely sparse.

- **At the start** of the Cambrian Period a rapid explosion of life forms occured. Trilobites and many other invertebrates were suddenly numerous.

- **In the Jurassic Period** (206–142 million years ago) sea urchins suddenly developed and evolved.

◀ *Charles Darwin was one of the first scientists to publish a theory of evolution of organisms.*

- **Charles Darwin's** famous book on evolution *The Origin of the Species*, was published in 1859. His theories of natural selection and the survival of the organisms best suited to a certain habitat are still accepted by most scientists today.

- **Modern scientists** are trying to increase our knowledge of evolution. Darwin didn't have access to new scientific ideas about DNA and genetics.

- **Mutation** is one of the keys to evolution. It is a change in the DNA of an organism, which may occur because of chemical or environmental influence.

- **Humans have influenced** the evolution of various organisms. Where industrial pollution has produced dark, grimy tree trunks, a dark form of the peppered moth has evolved, which is camouflaged in this habitat. Human misuse of the environment has driven many species to extinction.

Tracks, trails and burrows

- **Sedimentary rocks** can be formed as layers on the seabed, the land surface, a lake or river bed. These layers (strata) were at one time the Earth's surface, and they often have puzzling grooves and trails running over them.

- **Along with a wide range** of other structures, these trails are called trace fossils.

- **A fossil**, the record of past life, does not have to be a shell, bone or leaf. It can be a burrow, track, eggshell or dropping that tells us that a creature or plant has existed.

- **The study of** these trace fossils is called ichnology.

- **Trace fossils** are given scientific names, like other fossils.

- **Some of the most famous** trace fossils are dinosaur footprints. These can be used to work out the size and speed of a dinosaur.

▲ *These narrow grooves were probably made by molluscs moving over wet mud on the Carboniferous seabed.*

- **For a trace fossil**, such as a burrow or arthropod track, to be preserved, it must be filled in with mud or sand very soon after it is made, or it will be washed away.

- **In some cases**, the fossil of the mollusc or shrimp that has made a trace fossil is found at the end of its fossil burrow.

- **Dinosaur eggs** are trace fossils. Nests of *Protoceratops'* eggs and young have been found in Mongolia.

- **A trace fossil** called *Cruziana* occurs in many strata of Palaeozoic and Mesozoic age. Originally, it was thought to be the trail of a trilobite, but these arthropods became extinct in the late Palaeozoic. It is possible that a number of different arthropods made very similar trails.

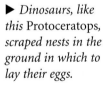

▶ *Dinosaurs, like this* Protoceratops, *scraped nests in the ground in which to lay their eggs.*

Rocks made of fossils

- **Some sedimentary rocks** are made almost entirely of fossils and fossil fragments.

- **Coal**, which has been one of the most important fuels since the 1800s, is made of the altered fossil remains of plants.

- **The finest fossils** are usually found in rocks that are made of very small particles of sediment. These are able to preserve details. Also, such sediment is less likely to crush the original organism as it is buried.

- **There are a number** of types of limestone that are classified as organic limestone, meaning that they are largely made of fossil remains.

- **Crinoids** are marine organisms related to starfish and sea urchins. They are made of calcite, and have a long, brittle stem that raises the animal off the seabed. Their broken remains, stuck together with lime mud, make crinoidal limestone – common in the Carboniferous system.

- **Chalk** is a very fine-grained, almost dusty, limestone, mainly formed during the Cretaceous Period, 142–65 million years ago. It is made of countless minute fossils, including coccoliths.

- **Coral reefs**, not unlike those that occur today, have existed at many times during the past. These reefs, rich in brachiopods, trilobites, molluscs and corals, are sometimes preserved as fossil-rich limestone.

- **Shelly limestone** is a term used by geologists for a rock composed mainly of fossil shells. These may be of molluscs or brachiopods (lampshells).

- **Shelly limestones** may once have been banks of shells washed together by sea currents.

- **Even when** there seems to be no fossils in a rock, it may still be made largely of fossil fragments. The use of a x10 hand lens will show this.

◀ *The chalk in this cliff is almost entirely composed of fossil material, mainly tiny sea organisms called coccoliths.*

Microfossils

- **Microfossils** are tiny fossils that can only be studied with the help of a microscope. There is no actual agreed size below which a fossil is considered a microfossil. When seen at high magnification, microfossils reveal a remarkable array of shapes and structures.

- **The larger fossils**, such as shells, bones, teeth and plant remains, are called macrofossils.

- **Microfossils are widespread** and commonly overlooked. Most sedimentary rocks contain microfossils, and a study of these can give important details about the age and environment in which the rock was formed.

- **Many microfossils** are of single-celled organisms, and the use of an electron microscope is necessary to study them.

- **The study** of fossil pollen, palynology, is a branch of micropalaeontology. Pollen is a very good indicator of past climates.

- **The pure-white** limestone called chalk is made up of microfossils including coccoliths. These are single-celled, planktonic organisms with a circular structure. They are most numerous in warm seawater.

- **At certain points** in the geological record there are rocks referred to as cherts. These are silica-rich sediments, some of which are formed by accumulations of microfossils called *Radiolaria*.

- **Conodonts** are minute, toothlike fossils. Exactly what they are has been a matter of discussion. Studies of complete conodont fossils suggest that it may have been an eellike creature. They only occur in rocks from the Cambrian to Triassic ages.

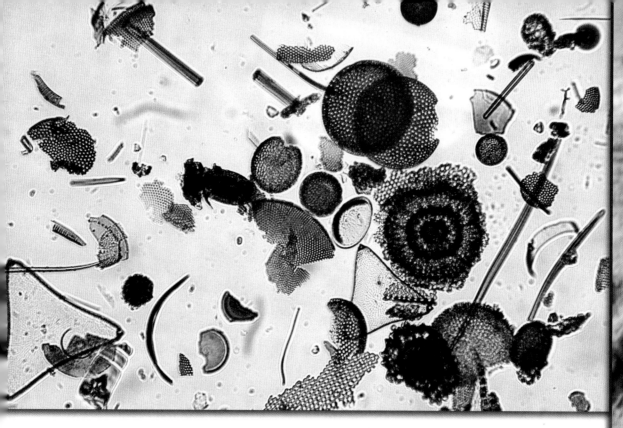

▲ *Among the commonest fossils are minute microfossils. These diatoms (minute, single-celled algae) are magnified many hundreds of times.*

- **Foraminifera** are single-celled organisms that live as plankton or on the seabed. Their tiny shells make up much of the 'ooze' that covers the deep ocean floor.

- **Nummulites** are slightly larger types of Foraminifera that often make up nummulitic limestone. This rock was used a lot as a building stone in ancient Egypt.

The oldest fossils

- **The record of fossils** from Pre-Cambrian times (4600–545 million years ago) is remarkably sparse. This is most of geological time, and yet we know very little about what was alive then.

- **Pre-Cambrian rocks** are often changed by metamorphism, and so any fossils they may have contained could have been removed.

- **Primitive life forms** would have had soft bodies, probably without shells, so may not have been preserved as fossils.

- **In its early years**, the Earth's atmosphere lacked oxygen and may have been composed of gases such as water vapour, methane and ammonia. These are not useful to life as we know it today.

◀ *During the end of the Pre-Cambrian Period many organisms developed, including these fronds of* Charnia, *probably a sea pen.*

- **Life probably** first developed around 3500 million years ago, though there is very little fossil evidence from this time.

- **Among the earliest** fossils are 3500 million-year-old algal remains found in Western Australia.

- **In the silica-rich** chert near Lake Superior in the US, fossil microscopic plant cells occur, suggesting that there was more oxygen about.

- **Late in the Pre-Cambrian**, organisms became more numerous. One of the most famous groups of fossils, the 'Ediacaran assemblage', comes from a number of sites, including Australia, England, Newfoundland, Scandinavia, Russia and Africa.

- **Ediacaran fossils** include delicate organisms such as jellyfish, worms, frondlike organisms and sea pens.

- *Charnia* is a famous Ediacaran fossil found in 1957 in Charnwood Forest, Leicestershire, by a schoolboy.

27

Fossil algae

- **Though they are very delicate organisms**, certain algae build calcium carbonate structures that are easily preserved as fossils.

- **The best-known fossil** algal structures are called stromatolites, made by blue-green algae.

- **Algae and bacteria** work together to build the rounded mounds of layered calcium carbonate.

- **When seen in a rock face**, stromatolites are mounds of calcite. On a flat surface they look like concentrically banded discs.

- **The earliest stromatolites** are found in rocks over 3000 million years old.

- **In the 1950s**, living stromatolite-building algae were found in Western Australia. Here they exist in water that is highly saline, where other organisms can't survive.

- **Much Pre-Cambrian** limestone is the result of stromatolite formation.

- **Blue-green algae** produce oxygen. This vital gas began to accumulate in the Earth's early atmosphere, allowing evolution to develop oxygen-dependent organisms.

- **This abundance of oxygen** led to the formation of the ozone layer high in the atmosphere, which protects us from harmful ultra-violet radiation.

- **Stromatolites** have occured on Earth for thousands of millions of years.

◄ *Stromatolites such as these are found fossilized in rocks 3000 million years old. Similar organisms live today in Australia.*

Primitive plants

- **The first vascular plants** (plants with veins) evolved in the late Palaeozoic Era.

- **In Devonian rocks** there is evidence of a rapid evolution of plants, and the Earth's surface began to look green for the first time.

- *Cooksonia* is a very early veined plant and occurred in rocks of late Silurian and Devonian age. During this period there were large landmasses on which vegetation could develop.

- **With a stiff stem**, *Cooksonia* could stand up above the surface, in which it was held by primitive roots.

- **Like modern plants**, *Cooksonia* had xylem cells that were able to transport water through the plant.

- **The fossil plant** *Parka* is also from the Devonian Period. Both *Cooksonia* and *Parka* probably reproduced with spores.

◄ *This reconstruction of* Cooksonia *shows its delicate branching stems and fruiting masses.*

▲ *These slender stems of* Cooksonia, *one of the first land plants, were found in rocks of Devonian age in Orkney, Scotland.*

- **Like many fossil plants**, these early Devonian species are preserved as thin carbon films, the rest of the plant tissue being lost during fossilization.

- **One of the best** examples of early plant preservation is a rock formation called the Rhynie chert, found in Devonian rocks in Scotland. Here, early plants are preserved three-dimensionally in silica.

- **Microscope analysis** of these silica fossils shows all their soft parts, allowing cellular structures to be examined.

- **It is probable that the Rhynie chert** was deposited by hot springs, the plant remains washing in from nearby.

Fossil plants and coal

- **When plants grow**, their energy is largely obtained from sunlight, which they use for photosynthesis and tissue development. This energy is locked away, but is released when coal formed from plants is burnt.

- **Coal is formed** when plant material is buried, compressed and heated.

- **The most important** deposits of coal, formed in the Carboniferous Period, occur in the UK, North America, Belgium, France, Australia and Siberia.

- **Coal of Permian**, Triassic and Jurassic age is important in China, Europe and the USA. Coal from the Jurassic Period can be found in parts of the UK, especially northeast Scotland.

- **As coal is formed** from advanced land plants, no coal of any value built up before Carboniferous times, when vast forests grew in the swamps.

- **Carboniferous coal-forming forests** grew in warm, sub-tropical areas where rainfall was high, allowing rapid growth of giant horsetails and clubmosses.

- **The development** of brown, damp peat is the first stage in coal formation.

- **Peat is used as a fuel** in many parts of the world, but it doesn't burn at such a high temperature as coal.

- **In Ireland**, and many other countries including Russia, there are power stations that generate electricity by burning peat.

- **As peat is buried** under thousands of metres of sediment, it is heated and all impurities are removed. This increases the percentage of carbon, and turns the peat into coal.

▼ *Swamp forests, which produced coal, developed at many times in the past. This reconstruction shows a forest of Jurassic age.*

33

Coal-forming plants

- **The richest deposits of coal** have been formed by the accumulation of peat from forests. Coal-forming forests flourished in the Carboniferous Period.

- **As these forests grew** on the swampy top of vast deltas, they were flooded by the sea numerous times. This flooding brought sand and silt onto the deltas, in which fossil plants are often preserved.

- **A great variety of plants** grew in Carboniferous forests, including giant horsetails, clubmosses and seed ferns.

- *Lepidodendron* is a common fossil clubmoss from Carboniferous strata. It grew to over 30 m in height. The roots of this clubmoss are usually found as separate fossils, and are called *Stigmaria*.

- *Lepidodendron* stems can be recognized by their diamond-shaped leaf scars.

- **Another common** Carboniferous coal fossil is the giant horsetail, *Calamites*. Today, horsetails are relatively small plants that live in damp ground. *Calamites* grew to around 30 m tall.

- **Horsetails** have soft tissue inside their stems, which decays rapidly when they die. During fossilization, the stems often filled with sediment, so they are preserved in three dimensions.

- **A group of smaller plants** that helped make coal were called seed ferns.

- **Seed ferns** are plants with fernlike leaves, often preserved as carbon films on bedding planes.

- **Common Carboniferous** seed ferns include *Neuropteris*, *Eupecopteris* and *Sphenopteris*.

▼ *These alternating coal, shale and sandstone strata are on the coast of Fife, Scotland. The darker layers are coal made from plants that grew in the Carboniferous delta forests.*

Mazon Creek, Illinois

- **At certain times** in the fossil record a number of remarkably detailed accumulations of fossils occured.

- **At Mazon Creek in Illinois**, coal has been strip-mined for many tens of years. Above the coal layers there are mudstones, in which rounded, iron-rich lumps, called nodules, occur.

- **Nodules like these** are common in mudstone and shale of different ages. Their importance is that fossils contained in them are often beautifully preserved in great detail.

- **It is thought** that these, and nodules in other strata, often form chemically around organic remains.

- **Plant fossils**, especially leaves, are commonly crushed on bedding planes, but in the Mazon Creek nodules, leaves are three-dimensional.

▶ *The delicate leaflets of the seed fern* Neuropteris *have been preserved as a carbon film inside an iron-stone nodule.*

◀ *None of the original carbon remains in this specimen of* Eupecopteris, *another seed fern. Nodules have to be opened very carefully to reveal such fossils.*

- **As well as perfect plants**, these rocks contain an amazing variety of other fossils, and geologists can work out the details of the habitats in which they lived.

- **Marine and fresh-water** creatures are found here. Fossils of jellyfish (only preserved in ideal circumstances), worms, amphibians and fish all occur in the Mazon Creek strata.

- **As often occurs** in cases of exceptional fossilization, there are fossils of soft-bodied creatures that are otherwise unknown.

- **Other examples** of nodules containing exceptional fossils are those from the Carboniferous rocks of Lancashire, and the ammonite-bearing nodules of the British Lower Jurassic.

...FASCINATING FACT...

Spiders, scorpions, centipedes and millipedes are fossilized at Mazon Creek, giving us a glimpse into a Carboniferous world that is unknown elsewhere.

Glossopteris and Continental Drift

- *Glossopteris* is an extinct seed fern. Its fossils occur in the southern landmasses of Antarctica, Australia, New Zealand, South America and southern Africa.

- **This plant** had a treelike appearance and was up to 6 m tall.

- **Usually only** the delicately veined leaves are found as fossils.

- **One of the most famous** geological books is *The Origins of Continents and Oceans*, written by Alfred Wegener, and published in 1924.

- **In this book**, Wegener puts together evidence to prove that the southern continents were at one time joined as a single landmass and have now drifted apart to their present positions.

- **Wegener was not a geologist** but a meteorologist, and his ideas were initially dismissed by the leading geologists of the time.

- **Because** *Glossopteris* occurs in the southern continents, which are now hundreds of miles away from each other, Wegener was able to use it as one of his key pieces of evidence to show that these areas had once been joined.

- **The problem** when he put forward his theory was that it was not understood how the continents could move.

- **Today** we have the knowledge of plate tectonics, which shows how the ocean basins form and how the continents move, proving that Wegener was correct.

▶ Glossopteris *grew to around 6 m in height. It may have grown with a treelike or bushy habit.*

- **The theory of plate tectonics** shows that the continents move at about 2.3 cm a year, the same speed at which your finger nails grow.

▲ *These iron-stained* Glossopteris *leaves are from Australia.*

Ginkgo and other living fossils

- **The expression 'living fossil'** is often used to describe a plant or animal that occurs as a fossil in rocks formed many millions of years ago, and also lives today.

- **Living fossils** have been changed very little by evolution and have a very stable habitat and way of life.

- *Ginkgo biloba*, the maidenhair tree, is grown in many countries, including the UK, as an ornamental tree, and is prized for its medicinal properties.

▶ *A leaf from the modern maidenhair tree,* Ginkgo biloba, *is very similar to the Jurassic fossil leaves.*

- **In China**, *Ginkgo* was cultivated in temple gardens as a sacred tree. It was thought to be extinct until some were found in the wild in southeast China in 1956.

- **Leaves of *Ginkgo***, usually preserved as carbon impressions, have been fossilized in rocks from the Permian Period (290–248 million years ago).

- **Fossilized *Ginkgo*** leaves are virtually the same as those of the living tree.

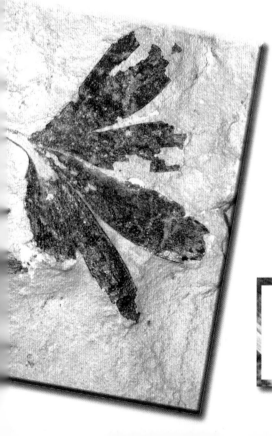

- **The leaves of** *Ginkgo* are very distinctive, being almost triangular in shape and partly indented.

- **Some of the best** *Ginkgo* fossils are from Jurassic strata on the coast of North Yorkshire, UK.

- **The brachiopod shellfish** *Lingula*, occurs in rocks of Cambrian age (545–495 million years ago). It is one of the earliest examples of a living fossil.

◄ *Leaves of* Ginkgo *from Jurassic strata in North Yorkshire, UK.*

. . . FASCINATING FACT . . .
Other well-known living fossils include the coelacanth, a fish thought to have been extinct for more than 60 million years until one was caught off South Africa in 1938.

41

Mesozoic and Cenozoic plants

- **Many ferns and fernlike plants** are fossilized in rocks formed during the Jurassic Period.

- *Coniopteris* is a fern found in Jurassic rocks. It occurs in North America, Europe and Asia.

▼ *These delicate leaves are from the fernlike Jurassic plant, Williamsonia, which flourished in the swamp forests of the middle Jurassic Period.*

...FASCINATING FACT...
Flowers provide a way for plants to evolve, as pollen can combine
the genes of one plant with those of another.

- **Another common Jurassic** plant is *Williamsonia*. This is an extinct plant with fernlike leaves, which are usually preserved as black carbon films on bedding surfaces. It had cones rather than typical modern flowers.

- **The evolution** of flowering plants began towards the middle of the Mesozoic Era.

- **There is evidence** that plants with flower-like structures lived early in the Cretaceous Period (142–65 million years ago), but fossils of true flowers only occur towards the late Cretaceous.

- **Much of the evidence** that early plants bore flowers comes from fossil pollen.

- **Fossil pollen** is invaluable in helping to work out changes in the climate of the past.

- **The evolution of insects** is closely linked to the development of flowering plants. Insects feed on nectar and pollen, and carry pollen from flower to flower.

- **Fossil insects** are often perfectly preserved in amber, the hardened resin from pine and similar trees.

Fossil corals

- **Much limestone**, especially that deposited during the Palaeozoic Era, consists of fossilized corals and coral fragments.

- **The earliest corals** are simple 'tabulate' corals, which first appeared as fossils in rocks of the Ordovician Period.

- **Tabulate corals** have a tubular structure and may be attached to others to form a colony. The tube (corallite) is divided horizontally by sheets of calcite called tabulae.

- **The coral organism**, or polyp, was rather like a small sea anemone, and lived at the top of the tube.

- **Tabulate corals** became extinct in the Permian Period.

- *Dibunophyllum* belongs to a group called the 'rugose' corals. These are more complex than the tabulate group.

- **In the Silurian** and Carboniferous Periods, rugose corals built large, shallow sea reefs, in which numerous fossils of corals, brachiopods, molluscs, crinoids and trilobites are found.

  - **The rugose corals** became extinct at a similar time to the tabulate corals, in the Permian Period.

    - **Some corals** in the Carboniferous Period are used as zone fossils. Each coral species represents a small part of geological time.

      - **Modern corals** began to evolve early in the Mesozoic Era.

◀ *The delicate internal structure of corals is often well preserved in fossils, as seen in this species,* Dibunophyllum.

Lower Palaeozoic corals

- **Tabulate and rugose corals** flourished during the Lower Palaeozoic Era and at times built up large reefs.

- **Corals are easily fossilized.** They are made of calcium carbonate – the mineral calcite – which is stable in limestone. Also, they are solid structures, that are not easily eroded or broken.

- **Coral reefs** are good indicators of marine conditions and water depth. Their fossils help to reconstruct the ancient reef habitat.

- **Fossil molluscs,** brachiopods, trilobites, bryozoans and crinoids are also found in rocks formed in these reef habitats.

- *Halysites* is a tabulate coral with a colonial structure. Its common name is chain coral because the individual corallites are linked together in a chain.

- **Lime mud** was easily trapped within the structure of corals such as *Halysites*, and so limestone was able to form.

- **Some tabulate corals** grew as large mounds on the shallow seabed. *Favosites* is a colonial coral, with numerous small corallites joined in a honeycomb structure and is commonly known as honeycomb coral.

- **Both *Halysites* and *Favosites*** are common in reef limestones formed during the Silurian Period.

- **These corals** became extinct towards the end of the Devonian Period.

- *Halysites* **and** *Favosites* occur in many parts of the world including the UK, North America, Asia and Australia, suggesting that shallow marine conditions were widespread.

▶ *A fossil of* Halysites, *a type of coral. Its chainlike structure is clearly visible.*

Time recording in the Palaeozoic

- **Fossils can be used** to help reconstruct ancient habitats and to work out details about geological time, which can sometimes be verified by astronomers.

- **A study** of modern corals shows that they build up layers of calcite at regular times.

- **Within these calcite bands** there are thicker monthly and annual accumulations of calcite.

◀ *Growth bands in* Ketophyllum *shows that there were probably more than 400 days in the Silurian year.*

- **Fossil corals** are often preserved in great detail. This is because the calcite layers of which they are composed are very stable in limestone, and little altered. Many coral reefs are preserved almost as they lived.

- **A detailed analysis** of fossil corals shows considerable differences in the numbers of growth layers from modern corals.

- **The coral *Ketophyllum***, which is fossilized in rocks of the Silurian Period, has 400 small growth bands between the wide annual markers.

- ***Lithostrotion***, a common colonial coral found in Carboniferous rocks, has 398 growth bands per year.

- **There were**, as seen from the coral evidence, 400 days in the year during the Silurian Period, and 398 days in the year during the Carboniferous Period.

- **The relationship** between the Earth and the Sun has been changing through geological time. Corals prove that each day is now longer than in the past.

...FASCINATING FACT...
There are often 360 calcite secretions built up each year on modern corals, suggesting almost daily growth.

Jurassic reefs

- **The corals that evolved** during the Mesozoic Era, in the shallow sea reefs of the Jurassic Period, were different from those of the Palaeozoic Era.

- **Jurassic corals** are classified as Scleractinian corals. They are also called hexacorals, because they have six internal divisions.

- **Scleractinian corals** have many similarities to corals that live in tropical seas today.

- *Isastrea* **is a typical Jurassic coral** that flourished in warm, clear seawater with little mud suspended in it.

- **Modern tropical corals** require similar conditions, if warm, clear water through which sunlight can penetrate.

- *Isastrea* grew as a mass of small, joined, individual corallites standing upright on the seabed.

- **When a lot of muddy sediment** was deposited, the coral reefs died out.

- **Lime mud** formed around corals that often derived from broken shells and other fossil debris. This then turned into limestone.

50

- **Many molluscs** thrived in this reef environment. Ammonite shells are also found in these limestones.

- **Other common fossils** in the reef rocks include brachiopods and burrows made by shrimps.

◀ *This specimen of* Isastrea, *from the Jurassic Period, shows the individual six-sided corallites.*

Fossil sponges

- **Sponges are mostly marine animals** that live in various habitats, and can be found today in low-shore rock pools.

- **Sponges are delicate organisms**. They are among the simplest multi-celled creatures.

▶ *This modern tropical vase sponge has a feather star growing on it. Feather stars are closely related to starfish and sea urchins*

▶ Raphidonema *is a fossil vase sponge common during the Mesozoic Era.*

- **A sponge** is made of a thin, porous structure, which is supported by small spines called spicules. Spicules are sometimes made of silica, a resistant material that may make up certain rock materials such as chert.

- **Surprisingly**, despite their structure, sponges are not uncommon as fossils.

- **Fossil sponges** occur mainly where sediment was deposited in a calm marine environment, with no strong currents.

- **Rocks** as old as the Cambrian Period contain fossil sponges.

- *Raphidonema* is a well-known fossil sponge found in Mesozoic rocks.

- **Some fossil sponges**, including *Siphonia*, have long stems and stand on the seabed. They look like tulips.

- *Raphidonema* has a structure like a porous, crinkled vase. It grew from the seabed, with its wide opening pointing upwards.

- **Sponges form** part of a community of marine creatures. Often there are fossils of bivalve molluscs such as oysters and pectens, and also gastropods and ammonites found with the fossil sponges.

Fossil crinoids

- **Crinoids are strange animals**, which have a plantlike structure. They have roots, a stem and a cup (calyx) at the top, in which the animal lives.

- **Because of their structure**, crinoids are also called 'sea lilies'.

- **The solid parts** of the structure are made of calcite, which means crinoids are easily fossilized. However, it is usually only the stem that is preserved.

- **The stem is composed** of numerous small discs called ossicles. Before and during fossilization, the stem of a crinoid often breaks. Some crinoidal limestone is composed almost entirely of ossicles.

- **Above the calyx** are flexible, feathery arms. These direct water currents containing food towards the animal.

- **Crinoids** are closely related to starfish and sea urchins. All three groups of creatures belong to the phylum Echinodermata.

- ***Traumatocrinus***, from the Triassic rocks of the Ghizou Province, of China, shows the flexible stems and calyx with waving arms.

- **Crinoids** first evolved during the Ordovician Period.

- **Not all crinoids live** attached by their roots to the seabed. Some are free-swimming.

- **Today**, crinoids live in all depths of seawater. Some are even found in the deepest abyssal water.

▶ *Each of these specimens of* Traumatocrinus *has a calyx, arms and stem.*

54

Encrinus and the Triassic of Germany

- *Encrinus* is one of the best-preserved fossil crinoids. It reveals a lot about crinoids and their way of life.

- **During the Triassic Period**, much of Germany was covered by the sea. This was in great contrast to the dry, desert-like conditions that existed in Britain at that time.

- **Part of this German sea** is called the Muschelkalk. This name refers to the limestone rich in fossil shells, which formed there.

- **Crinoid fossils**, especially Encrinus, are abundant in the Muschelkalk limestones.

- **An important feature** of these fossils is the excellent preservation of the upper structure of the crinoids, the calyx.

- *Encrinus* has a perfect five-fold symmetry, as do many of the members of their phylum.

Calyx made of larger plates

Arms made of smaller
interlocking plates

- **Among its close relatives** are starfish and sea urchins.

- **These crinoids** have been studied for hundreds of years, and the name *Encrinus* was first used in the 16th century.

- **By comparing *Encrinus*** with living crinoids, its way of life can be suggested.

- *Encrinus* probably lived in flowing sea currents, with its calyx pointing into the current. This allowed food particles to be easily carried towards the animal.

◀ *This typical specimen of* Encrinus *shows the calyx, made of large plates, with the arms, made of smaller interlocking plates, folded tightly above.*

Jurassic crinoids

▲ *The slender arms of this specimen of* Pentacrinus *have been preserved in pyrite (fool's gold).*

- **During the Jurassic Period**, shallow seas existed at certain times in many areas, including Britain.

- **The crinoid** *Pentacrinus* is found fossilized in the limestones that were formed on this shallow seabed.

- *Pentacrinus* is well-known for the structure of its stem. The small ossicles, of which it is made, are star shaped. Because the stem is very brittle, these small stars are often all that is fossilized of the whole crinoid.

- **As well as being found** in limestones, *Pentacrinus* occurs in the dark mudstones formed in deeper parts of the Jurassic sea.

- **It has been suggested** that *Pentacrinus* may have lived on driftwood and other debris, as well as on the seabed. This could explain how it reached deeper water.

- **Modern species** of *Pentacrinus* are anchored to the seabed when they are young. As they mature, they break away and become free-swimming.

- *Pentacrinus* has very long arms rising above the small calyx. These arms branch many times.

- **When found fossilized** in dark mudstones and shales, *Pentacrinus* is often preserved in iron pyrite. This is an iron sulphide mineral with a glistening golden colour. It is known as 'fool's gold'.

- **Many other fossils** are found in the same strata as *Pentacrinus*. These include various molluscs, brachiopods and other echinoderms.

- **From a study of the rock** in which these fossils are found, and of the fossils themselves, the habitat can be reconstructed.

Brittle stars

- **Brittle stars** are delicate starfish with long, slender arms. Usually there are five arms, giving them typical echinoderm symmetry.

- **As in other starfish**, the animal's mouth is in the central disc. The flexible arms allow the creature to move rapidly over the seabed.

- **Many brittle stars** feed on plankton, but some species eat small shellfish.

- **Fossils** of brittle stars, which are scientifically called ophiuroids, are found in rocks dating as far back as the Ordovician Period.

- **There are a number** of 'starfish beds' in the fossil record, some of the best being found in lower Jurassic rocks.

- **Other numbers** of brittle stars have been found in Devonian rocks in Germany and Silurian strata in Scotland.

- **Today**, brittle stars often live in large numbers in both shallow and deep seas.

- **Because brittle stars are so delicate**, the possibility of them being washed together by sea currents and fossilized as a large number of perfect specimens is remote.

- **For a mass of brittle stars** to be fossilized together, it is likely that a colony was rapidly covered with mud or sand.

- **It has been discovered** that living brittle stars cannot escape from sediment more than 5 cm deep.

▶ *This fossil mass of brittle stars shows the central disc and flexible arms, all with five-fold symmetry.*

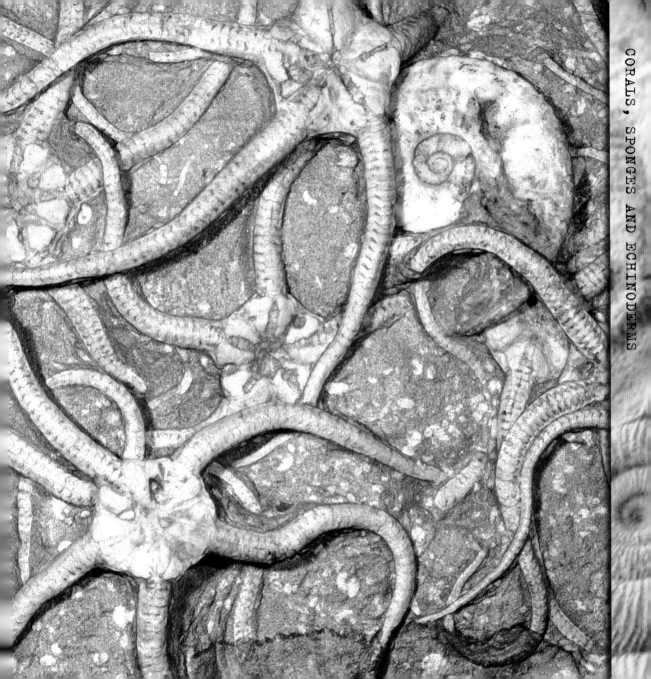

Jurassic sea urchins

- **Sea urchins** (echinoids) have evolved into many forms that are closely related to their habitat.

- **Regular echinoids** generally have a rounded shell (test). The mouthpart is positioned at the bottom of the shell, and the anus is positioned at the top.

- **The shell** is made of five bands of plates, which give it a five-fold symmetry. Spines are attached to the outside of the shell, and thin, delicate tube feet protrude through pores. The spines and tube feet are used for movement.

- **Irregular echinoids** have a similar structure but the shell has a two-fold symmetry.

▲ *This echinoid is called a 'pencil urchin' because of the size and shape of its spines. The ball-and-socket joints where they join the shell (test) are clearly seen.*

Hundreds of years ago in Oxfordshire, fossils of *Clypeus* were referred to as pound stones and used as a measure of weight.

- **Some echinoids** are flattened, like *Clypeus* while others are dome-shaped.

- *Clypeus* is a relatively large fossil sea urchin at about 10 cm in diameter.

- *Clypeus* has petal-shaped bands of plates running around its shell.

- **Modern sand dollars** are flattened echinoids, with similar shells to *Clypeus*. They live on or in the seabed in calm seawater.

- *Clypeus* often occurs in oolitic limestone of Jurassic age. It is often fossilized with molluscs and brachiopods.

◀ Clypeus *is an irregular sea urchin. Its spines were probably removed by sea currents before it was fossilized.*

Spiny sea urchins

- **Sea urchins** use their spines for moving about and as protection from predators.

- **The spines** on sea urchins vary greatly. Some echinoids have a few stout, club-shaped spines and others have a mass of slender, pointed spines.

- *Cidaris* is a fossil sea urchin from rocks of Jurassic to Recent age.

- **On its shell**, *Cidaris* has large, rounded 'bosses' where the spines were attached with a ball and socket joint.

- **Often the shell breaks** up during fossilization, and the large spines are frequently found as individual fossils.

- *Cidaris* **has a rounded shell** with the mouth central below, and is classified as a regular echinoid.

- **In rocks of Jurassic age**, *Cidaris* is found in limestone strata with many other fossils. These include corals, brachiopods, molluscs and bryozoans.

▶ Psammechinus, also known as the green sea urchin, *is a modern sea urchin with many thin, sharp spines.*

- *Psammechinus* is a spiny sea urchin that lives today in shallow seas, and can be found in rock pools on the shore at low tide.

- **The spines** on *Psammechinus* are relatively large. They are attached to the outside of the shell in a similar way to those on the fossil *Cidaris*.

- **As with fossil sea urchins**, the spines break off *Psammechinus* when it dies. Empty shells washed up on the shore rarely have spines attached to them.

◀ *Delicate echinoid spines are rarely preserved as fossils. The Jurassic sea urchin* Cidaris *is very similar to the modern-day* Psammechinus.

65

Burrowing sea urchins

- **Sea urchins** that burrow into the soft sediment on the seabed are often heart-shaped in outline.

- *Micraster* is a common fossil sea urchin. It is found in chalk formed in the Cretaceous Period.

- **Because of its unusual outline**, *Micraster* is classified as an irregular echinoid.

- **Other features** that make it irregular are its very short, petal-shaped rows of plates, and the non-central position of the mouth and anus.

- *Micraster* has been the subject of many scientific studies. An evolutionary sequence of this genus has been worked out.

- **The chalk** in which fossils of *Micraster* are found, was formed as a fine mud on the seabed.

▲ *This specimen of the Cretaceous sea urchin,* Micraster *has the typical heart-shaped outline of a burrowing echinoid.*

- **Other fossils** found with *Micraster* include bivalve molluscs, sponges, corals, brachiopods and fish teeth.
- *Echinocardium* is a modern sea urchin that lives in shallow seas. It burrows into mud and sand.
- **This recent sea urchin** has a heart-shaped shell, very similar to that of *Micraster*.
- **Though *Echinocardium* is covered** with soft spines when alive, dead shells washed up on the shore are usually bare of spines.

◀ Echinocardium *is a common echinoid around the coast of Britain. Its scientific name means 'spiny heart'. It is a burrower, like the fossil* Micraster.

Brachiopods

- **Brachiopods** are marine shellfish that are very different from other shelled animals. They are classified in a phylum of their own and are commonly known as lampshells.

- **A typical brachiopod** has a shell made of two valves. Some brachiopods are able to open and close their shells to let in seawater containing food.

- **The two valves** of a brachiopod shell differ from each other. One valve has a hole in its pointed end through which a tough stalk sticks out. This stalk, called the pedicle, anchors the animal to the seabed.

- **Inarticulate brachiopods** are the most primitive, and were first found fossilized in Ordovician strata.

- *Lingula* is an inarticulate brachiopod, as it can't open and close its shell.

- **This brachiopod** burrows vertically into soft mud on the seabed.

- **Modern-day** *Lingula* can help palaeontologists suggest what habitat this brachiopod lived in before they became fossilized

- **Primitive brachiopods**, such as *Lingula,* have different shell compositions from other brachiopods. *Lingula*'s shell is made of phosphates and chitin – a similar material to human finger nails.

- *Lingula* is found fossilized in dark shales and mudstones with other brachiopods and bivalve molluscs.

...FASCINATING FACT...
Lingula is called a living fossil because it has remained virtually unchanged for 500 million years.

▲ *These shells of* Lingula *are preserved in strata of Ordovician age.*

Palaeozoic brachiopods

- **Brachiopods** still live today, but they were far more numerous in the past than they are now.

- **During the Carboniferous Period**, many brachiopods, including *Spirifer* and *Productus*, lived in the shallow seas that covered much of Europe and North America.

- *Spirifer* and *Productus* are called articulate brachiopods because they could open and close their shells.

- **The symmetry** of a brachiopod shell is different to that of a bivalve mollusc. A bivalve has two valves that are similar to each other. A brachiopod's two valves differ from each other.

- *Spirifer* has a small shell crossed with thick ridges called ribs. There is straight hinge line along which the shell opens.

- *Productus* is a different shape from *Spirifer*. It is more rounded, and some species grew quite large. *Gigantoproductus* commonly grew to 15 cm in width.

▲ *This specimen of* Spirifer, *from Carboniferous limestone shows the straight hinge line and radiating ribs.*

- **The shell** of *Productus* is covered with circular growth lines and thin radiating ribs.

- ***Productus*** often has a spiny shell, though the delicate spines break off easily during fossilization. These spines may have helped to anchor the shell in mud on the seabed.

- **Both of these brachiopods** are commonly found in limestone of the Carboniferous Period.

- **Other fossils** found with *Productus* and *Spirifer* include corals, trilobites and molluscs.

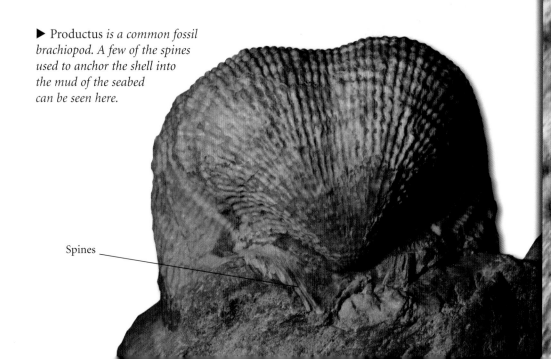

▶ Productus *is a common fossil brachiopod. A few of the spines used to anchor the shell into the mud of the seabed can be seen here.*

Spines

Rhynchonellids

- **Small brachiopods** with heavily ribbed shells are common in many Jurassic strata. These are classified as Rhynchonellids.

- **The shell** of a typical Rhynchonellid is only about 5 cm in diameter.

- **They are articulate brachiopods**, which could open and close their shells. The larger pedicle valve has a hole from which the fleshy pedicle protruded.

- **The shell** is made of calcite, unlike the phosphatic shell of the inarticulate brachiopods.

- **This group** seems to have been very successful, and first evolved during the Ordovician Period. Some species still live today.

- **A notable feature** of the shell is the zig-zag line along which the shell opens.

- **These brachiopods** are found in a number of different Jurassic strata. They are most common in limestones and ironstones, and also occur in sandstones.

1

KEY

1 Thecosmilia
2 Chlamys
3 Rhynchonellids
4 Rhabdophyllia
5 Bryozoan
6 Cladophyllia conybeari
7 Trochid

- **They are fossilized** with ammonites and other molluscs, crinoids, echinoids, and other types of brachiopods.

- **Rhynchonellids are often** fossilized in small clusters. It is probable that they lived attached in groups to the seabed.

- **From the strata** in which they are fossilized, it can be worked out that these brachiopods preferred clear seawater, without much sand or mud.

▲ *Small Rhynchonellid brachiopods lived attached to the seabed. In this reef habitat, numerous other organisms were common, including corals, molluscs and echinoids.*

Terebratulids

- **Though abundant** in Jurassic strata, the Terebratulid brachiopods have a very long geological history. They are still alive today, and the earliest fossils of them are found in Ordovician strata.

- **A typical Terebratulid** has an oval shell which is about 2.5 to 5 cm in length.

- **Often the shell is smooth**, without obvious ribs. Growth lines, which show the edge of the shell when it was smaller, can usually be seen.

- **One valve** is bigger than the other. This, the pedicle valve, has a hole for the pedicle.

- **Terebratulids**, like other articulate brachiopods, feed on material suspended in seawater. A current of water enters the shell when it is slightly opened.

- **Inside a brachiopod shell** is a structure called the brachidium. This is sometimes found in fossils. Its purpose was to support the main food-gathering organ, the feathery lophophore.

- **Terebratulid brachiopods** occur in a variety of Jurassic strata. However, they are most common in certain limestones.

- **Oolitic limestone** is a common rock formed in the Jurassic Period. It is made of minute, rounded grains of calcite that form in moving seawater.

- **Unlike the Rhynchonellids**, the Terebratulids occur individually, and seem not to have clustered in masses.

> ...FASCINATING FACT...
> Fossils found with Terebratulids include ammonites and other
> molluscs, corals, echinoids and crinoids.

▼ *The pedicle opening can be seen in this specimen, as a small hole filled with oolitic limestone. The wavy structure on the brachial valve is a fossil worm tube.*

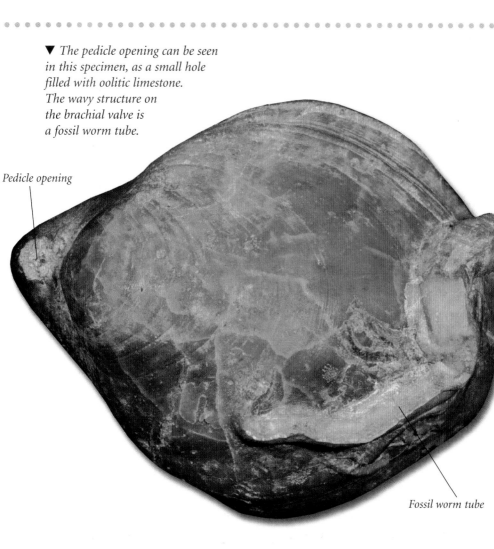

Pedicle opening

Fossil worm tube

Graptolites

- **Graptolites** were simple marine animals that first appeared in the Cambrian Period. They became extinct in the Carboniferous Period.

- **Graptolite** fossils are found in rocks that formed in the deep sea, such as dark mudstones and shales. The name 'graptolite' means 'writing in stone'.

- **A typical graptolite**, such as *Didymograptus,* has a slender, elongated structure, often only 2.5 to 5 cm in length. This is called the stipe.

- **When examined in detail**, a graptolite's stipe has a series of small projections on one or both sides, giving the appearance of the teeth found on a saw. These are called thecae, and in life were small cups in which tiny marine creatures called zooids lived.

- **The graptolite** is the structure built up by a colony of zooids and was either anchored to the seabed, or in other cases, floated on ocean currents.

- **Originally**, graptolites were classified with small colonial marine organisms called hydrozoans. In the 1940s, their classification was reorganized, when their biology was closely examined.

- **Graptolites are classified** in their own phylum, the Hemichordata, which also includes acorn worms and pterobranchs.

- **Because they are so delicate**, graptolites are preserved in only the finest-grained sedimentary rocks. They often occur in great masses, looking like pencil marks on the bedding planes.

- **Sometimes** they are preserved in iron pyrite, and three-dimensional preservation occurs in rare cases.

- *Didymograptus* is found in strata of Ordovician age.

▲ Didymograptus *can be identified by the 'V' shaped position of the two stipes. The saw-tooth thecae are on the inside of the 'V'.*

Graptolites and geological time

- **Though graptolites** are very delicate organisms, they are widespread geographically in certain strata from the Lower Palaeozoic Era.

- **Graptolites evolved** into many different species, and in some rocks are very common fossils.

- **A sequence of strata** has been established using graptolites as relative time markers (zone fossils). *Monograptus* is used as a zone fossil for rocks of the Silurian Period.

- *Monograptus* has a single stipe, with thecae only on one side, giving it the appearance of a miniature hack saw.

- **Graptolites** with thecae only on one side of the stipe are called uniserial graptolites. If the thecae are on both sides, they are called biserial graptolites.

- **Graptolites**, such as Monograptus, are believed to have been planktonic, carried by sea currents, while possibly attached to floating material.

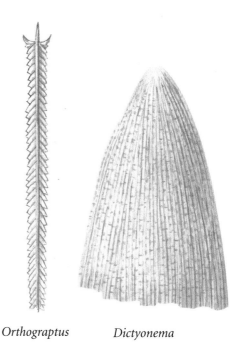

Orthograptus   *Dictyonema*

78

- **It is possible** that many planktonic graptolites would have drifted into areas where coarse sediment was deposited. Because graptolites are so delicate, they would have been crushed and destroyed as these rocks formed.

- **In some areas**, many thousands of *Monograptus* are fossilized on single bedding planes.

- **Some of the best-preserved** graptolites have been found in Silurian rocks in Germany and Poland. These rocks occur as boulders, slowly carried by glaciers from the bed of the Baltic Sea.

- **Perfectly preserved** graptolites can be removed from these boulders by dissolving pieces of the rock in acid.

▼ *Many different types of graptolites evolved. Some had single stipes, like* Monograptus, *others joined together in a colony, like* Dictyonema.

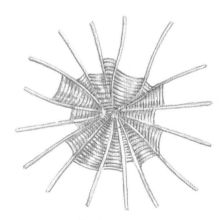

Monograptus   *Phyllograptus*   *Loganograptus*

79

Arthropods

- **Arthropods** are one of the most varied and successful groups of creatures to have evolved.

- **The first arthropods** are found fossilized in rocks of Cambrian age. They are still numerous in all manner of habitats today.

- **The scientific name** for the arthropod group is phylum Arthropoda. It contains creatures that can fly, swim, burrow and sting.

- **Butterflies and moths**, crabs and lobsters, shrimps, centipedes spiders and scorpions are all arthropods.

- **These creatures** have a tough outer skin (exoskeleton), which protects and holds together the soft body.

- **As an arthropod grows**, it sheds its exoskeleton. Many pass through a larval stage, and moult as the larva grows.

- **Some arthropods have claws**, others wings and most have segmented legs and thin, flexible feelers.

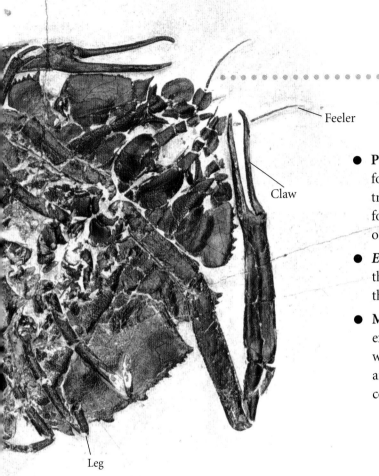

Feeler

Claw

Leg

- **Perhaps the best-known** fossil arthropods are the trilobites. Many trilobite fossils may be the remains of shed exoskeletons.

- *Eryon* is a marine arthropod that probably lived on the seabed.

- **Many arthropods** have excellent vision. Trilobites were the first known animals complex eyes that could form detailed images.

▲ Eryon *is an arthropod from Jurassic strata. It was an early member of the crab and lobster group, Decapoda. The segmented exoskeleton, legs, feelers and claws have been perfectly preserved.*

81

Giant sea scorpions

- **During the Palaeozoic Era**, arthropods called eurypterids (giant sea scorpions) terrorized the seabed.

- **The first eurypterids** appeared in the Ordovician Period, and became extinct in the Permian Period.

- **The largest** eurypterid grew to 2 m in length, however some were just 10 cm long.

- **These arthropods** had a tough outer skeleton, which they moulted as they grew.

- **The body was long and flexible**, and had six pairs of limbs. The pair nearest the tail were paddle-shaped, and were probably used for moving through the water.

▼ Pterygotus, *a giant sea scorpion, had good vision and large claws for grasping prey. At least one pair of limbs was adapted for swimming.*

▲ *This fossil sea scorpion,* Baltoeurypterus, *is from Silurian rocks in the Ukraine. It is shown here at life size.*

- **The head was small**, but in some kinds had huge, elongated claws extending from it.

- **Eurypterids** were good swimmers and relied on their long claws to grab prey.

- **Compound eyes** allowed these creatures to detect and catch their prey.

- **As well as** marine eurypterids, many other species also lived in brackish or fresh water.

Fossil insects

◄ This delicate fossilized mayfly is from rocks of Cretaceous age in Brazil. Even the wings have been preserved in the very fine-grained sediment.

- **Insects** have all the main features of the arthropods. Many of them are also able to fly.

- **Even though they are delicate**, insects have a tough exoskeleton. For this reason, the fossil record of insects is surprisingly good.

- **Insects often need** special circumstances to become fossilized. Very fine-grained, dustlike sediment helps to preserve delicate details.

- **Many insects** have been preserved in amber, the hardened resin that oozes from pine and similar trees. Insects that got stuck in the resin could become perfectly fossilized.

- **Because many insects** live on land, their fossils are less common than sea-dwelling arthropods.

- **Insects** first appeared as fossils in rocks of Devonian age.

- **During the Carboniferous Period**, giant dragonflies flew over the swamps that covered much of Europe and North America.

- **Some insects** pass through various stages of development (metamorphosis). Fossils of caterpillars and chrysalids have been found in rocks of Mesozoic age.

- **The first insects** were probably predators. When flowering plants developed in the Mesozoic Era, they provided pollen and nectar as food for many insects. In turn, insects carried pollen from flower to flower, and helped fertilize plants.

- **It has been suggested** that insect DNA could be recovered from fossils in amber. This is highly unlikely, as the chemical structure of DNA breaks down quickly.

Fossil crabs

- **As with other arthropods**, crabs have a hard outer skeleton, and moult as they grow.

- **The legs**, feelers and claws are attached underneath the body. Here, there is less exoskeleton and the crab may be more vulnerable to attack from predators.

- **Modern-day king crabs** are not crustaceans but chelicerates and are related to spiders and scorpions. They have a structure that is similar to that of the trilobites.

- *Mesolimulus* is a fossil king crab from Jurassic strata in southern Germany. It is very similar to certain modern king crabs.

- **The limestones** at Solnhofen, in which this and other delicate fossils have been preserved, are one of the most famous fossil deposits.

- **Other creatures** fossilized here include jellyfish, worms and arthropods such as shrimps and insects.

- **Mesolimulus** has a long tail spine and curved head shield.

- **Curved compound eyes** are positioned on each side of the head shield, and there are claws at the front.

- *Liocarcinus* is a
  typically modern
  fossil crab of the
  Crustacea group from
  Pleistocene strata at
  Rimini, Italy.

- **This crab** had a strong upper
  exoskeleton, often called the
  carapace, which allowed it to
  be preserved in sandstone.

◀ *With a tough carapace,
claws and legs, crabs are
quite easily fossilized. Here*
Liocarcinus *is preserved
in Pleistocene sandstone.*

87

Giant trilobites

- **Trilobites** are probably the best-known group of fossil arthropods. They are first found in rocks from the Cambrian Period.

- **Along with many different creatures**, trilobites became extinct during the Permian Period.

- **Trilobites** were advanced marine creatures, with a complex, three-lobed structure. They had a central axis and two lateral lobes, hence the name trilobite, which means three lobes.

- **They had a head shield** (cephalon), which in many types, including *Paradoxides*, had eyes. The central nervous system was probably here. *Paradoxides* had long spines extending back from the edges of the head shield.

- **The exoskeleton** was flexible, and *Paradoxides* was able to move across the seabed, using legs attached underneath.

- *Paradoxides* was a much larger trilobite. Its fossilized remains occur in Cambrian rocks in Europe, North and South America, and north Africa. It is used as a zone fossil to date rocks relatively.

- **It is a puzzle** to palaeontologists why creatures as complex and advanced as trilobites have no apparent ancestors. They are present in the Cambrian strata, but not before that.

- **Pre-Cambrian rocks** are often metamorphosed and altered, so any fossils in them would have been destroyed. However, there are marine sedimentary strata of late Pre-Cambrian times without any trace of trilobites in them.

- **Their ancestors** may have been soft-bodied creatures, which could not have become fossilized. Trilobites probably developed exoskeletons early in the Cambrian Period, and then would have been readily fossilized.

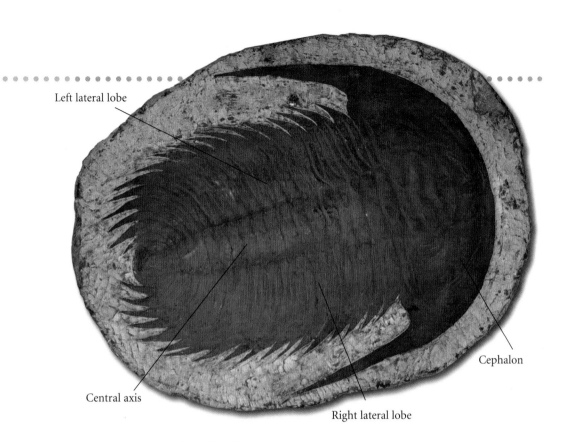

Left lateral lobe

Central axis

Right lateral lobe

Cephalon

▲ *This specimen of* Paradoxides *comes from early Cambrian strata in Morocco.*

...**FASCINATING FACT**...

Most trilobites were about 5 cm or less in length. *Paradoxides*, grew much larger, some giants were up to 60 cm long.

Silurian trilobites

▼ Trimerus *is a trilobite often found in limestone formed from Silurian reef deposits. In this rich habitat, molluscs, brachiopods and corals also thrived.*

- **During the Silurian Period** shallow marine conditions, with reefs, existed at certain times.

- **These reefs** were built up of lime-rich sediment that was bound together by many organisms, including corals and bryozoans. Between the reefs, limestone strata formed.

- **Conditions** at the time were favourable for many different organisms, and these rocks are rich in a variety of fossils. There are brachiopods, corals, molluscs and trilobites.

- *Trimerus* is an unusual trilobite from Silurian limestone. It has a very smooth carapace (upper exoskeleton), and the three-lobed structure is not easy to see.

- **The head shield** has a triangular outline, and there are no eyes.

- **The smooth** exoskeleton and lack of eyes suggest that *Trimerus* may have burrowed into the seabed mud.

- *Dalmanites* was a small Ordovician and Silurian trilobite, which had eyes raised above the head shield.

- **Trilobites with raised eyes** may have had good all-round vision. They may also have burrowed into the mud on the seabed, with their eyes protruding.

- *Dalmanites* has a typical trilobite structure, with three lobes and obvious head, thorax and tail sections.

- **In some species** of *Dalmanites* the tail section (pygidium) ends in a sharp spine.

Trilobite defence

- **The flexible outer skeleton** of many arthropods allows them considerable movement and some can roll up completely.

- *Calymene* is a trilobite from Silurian and Devonian rocks, and has many typical trilobite characteristics.

- **A strange feature** of *Calymene* is the two rounded projections on each side of the glabella (the central part of the head shield).

- **This trilobite** genus has a wide head shield, a typically three-lobed thorax and a small tail section.

- **As well as being found** as usual trilobite fossils, enrolled specimens of *Calymene*, and of other trilobites, have been found.

- **Many arthropods** including woodlice (pillbugs) can be found enrolled, with their hard carapaces protecting the softer parts hidden inside.

- **Like modern arthropods**, trilobites were probably able to enroll their bodies.

92

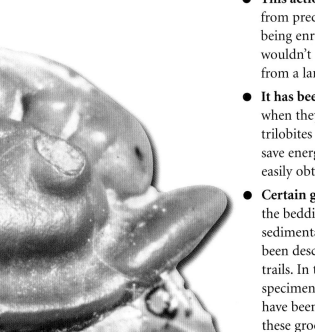

- **This action** provides a defence from predators. However, being enrolled probably wouldn't have saved a trilobite from a large predator.

- **It has been suggested** that when they were rolled up, trilobites would be able to save energy if food was not easily obtained.

- **Certain grooves** found on the bedding planes of some sedimentary rocks have been described as trilobite trails. In the USA, specimens of *Calymene* have been found near these grooves.

◀ *Trilobites may have rolled up in self defence. In this position the tough exoskeleton is outermost, protecting the softer body parts.*

Butterfly stones

▲ *A winged tail section (pygidium) of* Drepanura. *This limestone is also crowded with fragments of other fossils.*

- **Many trilobite exoskeletons** break up before they are fossilized. This usually happens between the head shield and thorax, and the thorax and pygidium (tail).

- **Moulted trilobite exoskeletons** may account for many of the fossils found. These may have broken as the trilobite wriggled out.

- **Fossil specimens** of *Drepanura* are usually only the tail sections. Only rarely are other parts of the animal found.

- **These fossils** are a very strange shape. They have a central section of small, toothlike spines and two extended spines on the edges.

- **Rocks containing** *Drepanura* often have many broken fragments of other fossils.

- *Drepanura* had eyes on its head shield.

- **Rocks** containing these fossils are often called 'butterfly stones', because of the winged shape of the pygidium.

- *Drepanura* is one of the earliest trilobites to be found in the fossil record, occurring in strata of Cambrian age.

- **As well as being found in China**, *Drepanura* also occurs in Cambrian strata in Europe.

...FASCINATING FACT...
Hundreds of years ago, probably before anyone knew what these strange shapes in the rocks were, they were collected and used by Chinese doctors. The Chinese called them 'Hu-die-shih'.

Very small trilobites

- *Agnostus* is one of the earliest trilobites, occurring in strata of Cambrian age.

- **As well as being a very small trilobite**, about 1 cm long, *Agnostus* has some unusual features.

- **This trilobite** has only two segments making up its thorax. The head shield and tail are both semi-circular.

- *Agnostus* had no eyes on the head shield.

- **In some areas**, great masses of broken exoskeletons of *Agnostus* are preserved as fossils.

- **Some of the most amazing Cambrian fossils** come from the Burgess Shale of British Columbia, and from Vastergotland in Sweden. In these areas, masses of strange, soft-bodied creatures and large numbers of crustaceans are preserved. These give us an idea of what life in the Cambrian sea was really like.

- **The predominance** of fossil trilobites, including *Agnostus*, in Cambrian rocks is probably a result of their hard exoskeletons being more easily preserved than the remains of soft-bodied creatures.

- **Fossils of *Agnostus*** have been found rolled up, like woodlice.

- **In well-preserved fossils** from Sweden, *Agnostus* trilobites have been found with an unusual appendage. This has made some palaeontologists wonder if *Agnostus* really is a trilobite.

- *Agnostus* **usually occurs** with fossils of other trilobites, molluscs and graptolites.

▶ *A mass of fragments of* Agnostus *trilobites preserved in limestone. Their typical length was 1 cm.*

Trilobite vision

- **Trilobites first appeared** in the Cambrian Period and unlike many of the creatures of the time, some were able to see.

- **Fossilized eyes** may seem a little strange, as eyes are soft and decay rapidly after death. Trilobites' eyes, however, were made of calcite (calcium carbonate), and could be easily fossilized.

- **Calcite** is a common mineral, which is found in many rocks, especially limestone. Under the right conditions, it can remain for millions of years in the Earth's crust, without being changed.

- **Trilobites** are related to many modern creatures with excellent eyesight such as dragonflies, flies, wasps, bees, crabs and lobsters.

- **Like many modern-day insects**, trilobites had compound eyes.

- **Human eyes** only have one lens, but compound eyes have many lenses all joined together.

- **Compound eyes** are excellent for seeing movement. For example, modern-day dragonflies can see smaller insects flying nearby and suddenly change direction to catch them.

- **Scientists** have tried to work out what a trilobite could see with its compound eyes. Many species probably had very good vision.

- **Some trilobites** had eyes on stalks extending from the head shield. They may have lived on the seabed, with their eyes sticking out of the mud like periscopes.

- **Not all trilobites had eyes.** Some used feelers and grooves in their exoskeleton for detecting the movement of water currents and finding their way about.

◄ Asaphus, *a type of trilobite, had eyes on raised stalks.*

Continental drift and trilobites

- **The theory of continental drift** suggests that the large land masses (continents) are constantly moving. At times during the past they have been joined together, though now many are separate.

- **A number of fossils** have been used to prove this theory, including the trilobite *Olenellus*. It can help to show that Scotland and North America were once joined together.

- **This trilobite** can be found in rocks from the Cambrian Period.

- **During the Cambrian Period**, North America and Scotland were joined. A deep ocean separated this area from Wales, and *Olenellus* was unable to move across it.

- **Although there are many places**, where Cambrian trilobites occur in Britain *Olenellus* is only found in north west Scotland.

- *Olenellus* is also fossilized in Cambrian rocks in North America.

- **The rocks** in which *Olenellus* is found were probably formed in relatively shallow marine conditions. These rocks include limestone and mudstone.

- **The main feature** that distinguishes *Olenellus* from other trilobites is its spines, which extend from the head shield and from the sides of the thorax and tail.

- *Olenellus* had large, curved eyes on the sides of the head shield.

- **It is an example** of an advanced Cambrian creature with no obvious pre-Cambrian ancestors.

▶ *A fossilized* Olenellus *trilobite from Cambrian rocks.*

Molluscs

- **Molluscs** live today in a great variety of habitats. They are very important fossils, occurring as far back as Cambrian times.

- **Molluscs** can live in both salt and fresh water. Some live on land, and some even climb trees. Fossil molluscs are good indicators of the habitat in which a layer of rock was deposited.

- **The word** 'mollusc' refers to creatures that have a soft, slimy body, which may or may not have a shell around it.

- **Molluscs** include octopuses, slugs and snails, clams and oysters, squids and cuttlefish, and tusk shells.

- **Scientifically**, the phylum Mollusca is divided into smaller groups called classes. Among the main classes are the Gastropoda, Bivalvia and Cephalopoda.

- **Some gastropods** (Gastropoda) can live in water, others on land. They are slugs, snails and limpets. This class is not as common in the fossil record as the other molluscs.

- **Bivalves** (Bivalvia) live in both salt and fresh water. Some bivalves, such as *Mya* (types of clam), burrow into sand and mud. *Pecten* (the scallop) can open and close its valves to swim, and oysters lie on the seabed.

- **The cephalopods** (Cephalopoda) are marine animals. They are amongst the most intelligent invertebrates, with a well-developed nervous system and sensitive eyes. Octopus, squid, cuttlefish and the pearly nautilus are in this class.

- **The ammonites**, one of the best-known groups of fossils, are classified as molluscs, and belong to the class Cephalopoda.

- **Molluscs** are common as fossils, sometimes occurring in such large numbers that they make up most of a sedimentary rock.

◀ *Ammonites are one of the best-known groups of extinct molluscs. They are common in strata of Mesozoic age.*

Bivalve molluscs that swim

◄ *This image shows the soft body of a scallop shell between the two valves. When the valves open and close, the animal swims in short bursts.*

● **These molluscs** are called bivalves because they have a shell made of two, usually similar, valves, which are a mirror image of each other.

● **Near the rounded** or pointed 'beak' of the shell (the umbo), there is a dark, horny, flexible ligament that holds the two valves together.

● **Just below the umbo**, on the insides of the shell, is a series of ridges (teeth) and hollows (sockets). Teeth in one valve fit into sockets in the other valve and, together with the ligament, make a hinge system.

● **Inside the shell**, the animal's body is surrounded by a fleshy membrane called the mantle.

● **Two strong muscles**, the adductor muscles, pull the valves together. When they relax, the valves open slightly.

● **Features** of the many fossil species of bivalves differ, often depending on the habitat in which the creature lived.

● *Pseudopecten*, from the Jurassic Period, and the modern *Pecten* (scallop) have one large adductor muscle. Although they are separated by many millions of years, their features are very similar.

- **These two bivalves** open and shut their valves using the large adductor muscle. This causes shellfish to swim in rather jerky movements through the sea.

- **In fossils** and empty modern shells, the point at which the adductor muscle joined the inside of a valve can be seen as a small, rounded indentation. This is the muscle scar.

- *Pecten* has a triangular shell with a pointed umbo. The valves are flat and strengthened with ribs.

▼ *This mass of shells is from the early Jurassic. They are very like modern scallops, and probably lived in a similar way, opening and closing their valves to swim.*

Fossil oysters

◄ *The wavy structure on this oyster shell is the edge of its fleshy body. Oysters have to open their shells so that they can feed.*

- **From the Mesozoic Era** to Recent times, oysters have been common marine shellfish.

- **Some fossil oysters** are very similar to those that live today, but others developed rather different shell shapes.

- **Unlike** most bivalve molluscs, oysters have valves that are not mirror images of each other. One of the valves is generally larger than the other.

- **Oysters** cannot move freely, and live on the seabed. They have a number of features that help them survive in shallow, turbulent water.

- **Usually** an oyster has very thick, heavy valves. These are adapted to being washed around by currents and tides, without being damaged.

- **The adductor muscle** is large and strong to hold the valves together when the shell is moved about by the sea.

- **As is typical of oysters**, *Gryphaea* had valves that are very different from each other. One valve was large and heavy, the other was thinner and smaller.

- **The larger valve** was hooked at one end and made of many layers of calcite.

- **This structure** probably allowed *Gryphaea* to lie on the seabed, with the heavy valve underneath. If disturbed by water currents, it would come to rest in this position again.

···FASCINATING FACT···
Because of its curved shape, *Gryphaea* is sometimes called the 'devil's toenail'.

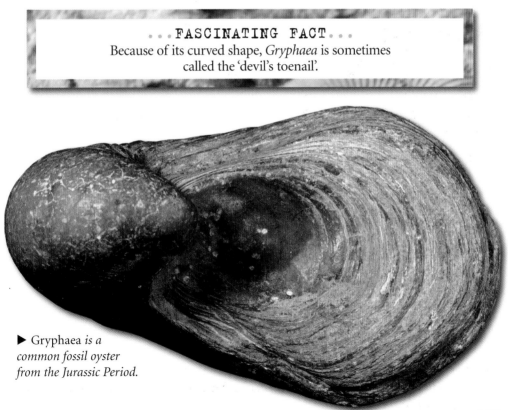

▶ Gryphaea *is a common fossil oyster from the Jurassic Period.*

Cenozoic bivalves

- **Many** of the marine bivalve molluscs that live today evolved during the Cenozoic Era.

- **Most of the shells** found on the beach are bivalve molluscs. Often the more delicate ones are broken, but some, especially those adapted to live on the seabed, may be washed up undamaged.

- **During fossilization**, especially in shallow water where coarse sediment such as sand is deposited, the strongest shells stand the best chance of being preserved.

- *Venericardia*, a type of clam occurs in Palaeocene and Eocene strata.

- **This bivalve** lived just below the surface of the mud or sand on the seabed, in a very shallow burrow.

- **It had a massive shell**, with strong ribs running across it to help withstand being disturbed and rolled around by sea currents.

- **The wide part** of the shell was in the upper part of the burrow, very near the sediment surface, so that it could feed from the water.

- *Arctica*, a living clam, is similar to *Venericardia*. It has a strong shell adapted to shallow conditions, and lives in a shallow burrow.

- **Although,** *Arctica* still survives today, it is also found fossilized in Eocene strata.

- **These two bivalves** rarely occur on their own as fossils. Usually the strata in which they are found contains many other bivalves, gastropods and fish teeth.

◀ Arctica *is a thick-shelled bivalve found in rocks from the Pliocene Epoch. It still lives today on the continental shelf, burrowing into sand and mud.*

109

Burrowing bivalves

- **Because** they are protected in their burrows, bivalves that tunnel into the seabed often have delicate shells.

- **Modern-day** bivalves such as *Mya*, clams and razor shells show typical features of burrowing bivalves.

- **Fossils of *Pholadomya*** are commonly found in strata of Jurassic age.

- **The shell** of this bivalve, and that of other burrowers, is often lengthened. The posterior end (the one furthest away from the beak or umbo) is stretched.

- **The modern razor shell** *Solen* is a good example of the lengthened shell. In this bivalve, the shell is virtually a long, flattened tube.

- ***Pholadomya*** is sometimes found fossilized in its burrow, positioned vertically in the strata, with the umbo downwards.

- **As they are confined** in a burrow, these bivalves cannot open and close their valves to feed. The upper end of the shell, the posterior end, is always slightly open. This opening is called the gape.

- **Two fleshy tubes** called siphons stick out of the open end of the shell above the seabed. One sucks water and food in, the other blows water and waste out.

- **In fossils**, or shells washed up on the shore, there is often a thin line inside the shell. This is called the pallial line, and marks where the edge of the animal's body joined the shell.

- **Burrowers** have a deep kink in the pallial line where the long siphons stuck out.

◀ *Modern razor shells burrow very rapidly into sand or mud on the seabed. This razor shell has its fleshy 'foot' extending outside the shell.*

Freshwater bivalves

- **Many bivalves** have adapted to living in fresh water. About one-fifth of bivalves living today are found in lakes and rivers.

- **In some cases**, where they are isolated geographically from other similar bivalves, new types have evolved.

- **Bivalves** that live in fresh water are different from their marine relatives.

- **Fresh water** does not hold as many shell-making chemicals as sea water does, so freshwater bivalves tend to have thinner, more delicate shells than marine ones.

- **Many different** freshwater bivalves are found fossilized in rocks of Carboniferous age.

- **During the later part** of the Carboniferous Period, much of Europe and North America was covered with river systems and deltas. Bivalve molluscs flourished in the streams and lakes on the deltas.

- *Carbonicola* is a typical inhabitant of Carboniferous waters. It is found fossilized in strata associated with coal beds.

- **This small bivalve** burrowed into the soft mud of streambeds.

- **Many years ago**, coal miners referred to the layers containing *Carbonicola* and other non-marine bivalves as 'mussel bands'.

- **Most bivalves** are not much use for the relative dating of rock strata. The bivalves that lived in the Carboniferous rivers and swamps can, however, help to link rocks geographically from place to place.

▲ *This thin-shelled bivalve lived in streams during the Carboniferous Period.*

113

Fossil gastropods

▲ Straparollus *moved slowly around the seabed, feeding. This specimen is from Carboniferous strata.*

- **Some gastropods**, such as snails and limpets, have shells. Others such as slugs have no external shells.

- **Gastropods** have evolved since the Cambrian Period, when they first appear as fossils.

- **Fossil gastropods** are not as common as fossil bivalves and cephalopods.

- **There are probably** more gastropods alive today than at any time in the past.

- **Gastropods** have adapted to many habitats. Some live in the sea, both crawling on the seabed and floating as plankton. They are also common on dry land.

- *Poleumita* is a typical sea snail from Silurian marine strata.

- **This gastropod** occurs in limestones deposited in shallow water, including those formed on reefs.

- *Poleumita* has a shell that coils in a low spiral. There are ridges and small spines on the shell.

- *Straparollus* lived from the Silurian to Permian Periods. It had a fairly smooth shell and lived in shallow seas.

- **Gastropods** such as these are often found fossilized with many other molluscs, brachiopods and corals. This shows that the habitat on the Palaeozoic seabed was favourable to life.

Cenozoic sea snails

- **During the Cenozoic Era**, gastropods began to develop different groups that still live today.

- **Fossil gastropods** often have their original shell intact, showing as much detail as a modern shell found on the beach.

- **Though fossils** of *Turritella* first occurred in rocks of Cretaceous age, it evolved into a number of species during the Cenozoic Era.

- *Turritella*, also known as towershell or turretshell, has a long, narrow shell with screwlike coiling. The fossil species are closely related to modern tower screw shells.

- **The coils** of the shell are called whorls. *Turritella* has a groove between each whorl.

- **The only details** on the shell are faint growth lines, which mark an earlier position of the shell opening.

- **Like many gastropods**, *Turritella* lived in shallow seas, and is found fossilized with other molluscs, corals and crustaceans.

- **Masses** of *Turritella* shells sometimes appear together, and make up a high percentage of the rock.

- **Modern species** of *Turritella* usually burrow into the mud and silt on the seabed. The sharp end of the shell points downwards and the opening is near the surface of the seabed.

- **It is probable** that fossil gastropods lived in a similar way. For them to be fossilized in large numbers, they must have been disturbed by sea currents and the shells washed together.

▶ *This mass of perfectly preserved* Turritella *shells is from Eocene strata in France.*

116

Predatory sea snails

- **During the Cretaceous Period**, gastropod molluscs were not as common as other groups, but in the Cenozoic Era they evolved rapidly.

- **Marine gastropods** developed many ways of feeding. Some became active predators.

- **Almost half** the number of fossilized gastropods found in rocks of Eocene age were predators.

- **These sea snails** were not very big, and many of them had sophisticated ways of killing and eating their prey.

- **Almost anything** living on the seabed would have been attacked by these snails. Sea urchins, molluscs and worms were all eaten. Some species even caught live fish.

118

- *Conus*, the cone shell was a typical predatory gastropod from the Eocene Epoch.

- **This small sea snail** had a very ornate shell, crossed by sharp ridges and lines. It is often fossilized in large masses.

- **Gastropods** have a radula, which is used for feeding. The radula is a sharp 'tongue' that is used to attack prey or rasp off plant material.

- *Conus* is found fossilized with many other molluscs, fish teeth, echinoids and corals.

...FASCINATING FACT...

Conus has a highly advanced radula that was like a thin harpoon. This was stuck into prey and then venom injected through a groove in the radula.

◀ *This modern cone shell shoots its poisonous radula into a whelk's shell. The venom is very powerful and quickly paralyzes the prey.*

119

Cephalopods

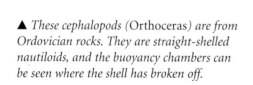

▲ *These cephalopods (Orthoceras) are from Ordovician rocks. They are straight-shelled nautiloids, and the buoyancy chambers can be seen where the shell has broken off.*

- **This class of molluscs** contains some of the most advanced invertebrates to have ever evolved.

- **The pearly nautilus**, octopus, squid and cuttlefish are all cephalopods, as well as many extinct groups such as ammonites and belemnites.

- **Modern cephalopods** have a highly developed nervous system and good eyesight.

- **All these creatures** live in the sea, and most are capable of free movement, often by jet propulsion.

- **As well as** squirting water for propulsion, many cephalopods can emit a cloud of dark, inky liquid, behind which they can hide from predators.

- **Both the external** and internal shells of cephalopods are common as fossils.

- ***Orthoceras*** is an early, straight-shelled nautilus, from lower Palaeozoic strata. The shell, like that of many cephalopods, is divided into chambers, with the animal living in the largest one at the open end of the shell.

- **Some species of *Orthoceras*** grew to several metres in length, though most were only a few centimetres long.

- **In some areas**, such as the limestone at Maquokota in Illinois, USA, large numbers of *Orthoceras* are found fossilized together.

- **Specimens** of *Orthoceras* limestone containing these fossils are cut and polished for ornamental use.

▼ *The modern octopus is a free-swimming mollusc that lacks an outer shell. It is a very advanced animal, with a complex nervous system and good eyesight.*

Devonian and Carboniferous cephalopods

- **In the upper Palaeozoic Era**, especially during the Devonian and Carboniferous Periods, cephalopods evolved with coiled external shells.

- **The coiled** shell had many chambers. At the wide end of the shell was the body chamber in which the squidlike animal lived.

- **Many smaller** buoyancy chambers extended back from the body chamber to the tightly coiled centre of the shell.

- **These chambers** may have been crushed on bedding planes during fossilization. In many cases however, they are preserved and infilled with crystals of minerals such as calcite.

- **Some cephalopod shells** are similar to a coil of rope, with all the coils (whorls) easily seen. This is called evolute coiling.

- **Shells** where the whorls overlap a great deal are said to have involute coiling.

- **The goniatites** are a group of cephalopods that lived in the Devonian and Carboniferous seas.

Suture line

- **Goniatites** may have been the ancestors of the Mesozoic ammonites and generally had involute shells.

- **The suture lines** have a zig-zag pattern and mark where the walls of the internal buoyancy chambers meet the outer shell.

- **The common**, free-swimming goniatites are used as zone fossils for marine strata of Devonian and Carboniferous age.

◀ *Goniatites are small cephalopods. The zig-zag suture pattern is clearly seen in this example from the Carboniferous Period.*

Modern and Jurassic nautilus

- **The pearly nautilus**, which today lives in the southwestern Pacific Ocean mainly around Australia and Indonesia, is regarded as a 'living fossil'.

- **Fossils** of similar species of nautilus occur in rocks dating back to the early Mesozoic.

- *Nautilus* has a broad shell with involute coiling. The inner whorls are largely hidden by the large outermost whorl.

- *Cenoceras* was a Jurassic nautilus, with many similar features to the modern pearly nautilus.

- **The suture lines** on a nautilus shell are gently curved, not zig-zagged, as in the goniatites, or complex, as in the ammonites.

- **Like many shelled cephalopods**, *Nautilus* has a large body chamber. The squidlike animal has numerous tentacles, eyes, and a funnel for squirting water, providing jet propulsion.

- **The smaller buoyancy chambers** are linked through their centres by a thin tube – the siphuncle. This allows the density of fluid and gas in the chambers to be regulated. The animal can thus control its depth in the sea.

◀ Cenoceras *had a large body chamber, and the inner coils of the shell are covered by the large outermost coil.*

- **The nautilus** has many biological differences from the extinct ammonites. However its shell is similar, and may give a good insight into how ammonites lived.

124

- **Because fossilized** nautilus shells span such a long period of time, they are little use as zone fossils.

- **Nautilus shells** are found washed ashore in east Africa and Madagascar, many hundreds of miles from where they live. Shells of dead ammonites could probably have drifted across the Mesozoic sea, thus enhancing their use as zone fossils.

▲ *The modern nautilus lives in the western Pacific Ocean, especially around Australia. It has good eyesight and moves by squirting out a jet of water.*

125

Ammonites

- **During** the Jurassic and Cretaceous Periods, ammonites evolved into a great variety of forms.

- **Ammonites** were marine creatures, and many could move freely in the water, though some of the largest may have browsed on the seabed.

- **The ammonite shell** is similar to the nautilus shell, but there are some very important differences.

- **The spiral coiling** of the ammonite shell does not usually extend upwards. It is coiled in a flat plane, with both sides of the shell depressed in the centre.

- **An ammonite shell** has a large body chamber at the shell opening. This chamber reaches back for about half a whorl. Usually the animal lived with the body chamber at the lowest point, and the rest of the shell above.

- **The smaller buoyancy chambers** are linked by a thin tube, called the siphuncle. This runs along the outside of each whorl, not in the centre as in the nautilus.

- **The buoyancy chambers** are separated from each other by walls called septa. Where these reach the shell, they become very complex. If some of the outer shell is worn away, or removed, these complex patterns are revealed as suture lines.

- **Ammonite shells** can be distinguished from nautilus and goniatite shells by their wavy, frilly or lobed suture lines.

- *Psiloceras* is one of the first ammonites to appear in rocks of Jurassic age. As ammonites are used as zone fossils, it marks the base of the Jurassic Period.

- **This ammonite** has a shell coiled mid-way between involute and evolute, and only faint ridges running across the whorls.

126

Whorl

Frilly suture lines

Body chamber

▶ *It is unusual to find uncrushed specimens of* Psiloceras. *These examples are from a boulder washed up on the shore of North Yorkshire, UK.*

Ammonite variety and movement

◀ This reconstruction shows the ammonite Lytoceras swimming in the warm Jurassic ocean. Ammonites had far fewer tentacles than the nautilus.

- **Fossil ammonite shells** show a vast range of different shapes, sizes and structures. The movement of different species may have depended on their shape.

- **Some ammonites** were big and round, others were thin and disc-shaped. Some had shells that were quite small, others very large.

- **The outer surface** of a fossil ammonite shell may be covered with ridges (ribs), spines and knobs.

- **Exactly** what function these features had is unknown. Ribs may have added strength to the shell, and spines may have helped protect against predators.

- **For an animal** that was able to swim, various features of the shell could have kept the ammonite in the correct position and helped with streamlining.

- **Scientists** have studied how the nautilus moves in order to try and suggest the swimming ability of ammonites.

- **Nautilus** can move both slowly and in rapid bursts by using the muscles in its large body cavity, and by squirting water from its funnel.

- **Ammonites** had a very different body chamber from that of the nautilus. In the ammonite shell, the part occupied by the animal's body was generally narrow and tube-shaped, though some did have wide body chambers. The nautilus has a wide, expanded body chamber.

- **It is thought that** most ammonites were poor swimmers, especially when compared with modern squids.

- **By altering the fluids and gas** in the buoyancy chambers, ammonites could regulate their density, and were able to change their depth in the water.

Ammonite suture lines

- **One of the most** striking features of fossil ammonites is the pattern of complex lines that can often be seen running across the shell. These are called suture lines.

- **The suture lines** do not occur on the outside of the shell, and must not be confused with the ribs or other external markings.

- **Suture lines** are on the inner surface of the shell. Only slightly worn shells, or shells where some of the outermost material is broken off, show these complex lines.

- **Each suture line** marks where an internal division between two chambers joined the inner surface of the shell.

- **This join** was very complicated, as shown by the pattern of the suture line.

- **Ammonite fossils** often break, and a small fossil may be only the inner whorls of a large ammonite, the body chamber and large outer whorls having been destroyed.

▲ *When polished, and the outer layer of shell removed from this* Eparietites, *the intricate suture lines can be clearly seen.*

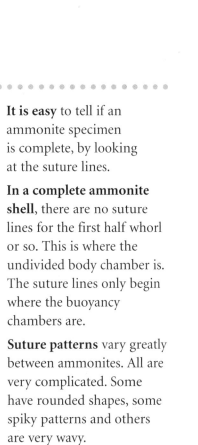

- **It is easy** to tell if an ammonite specimen is complete, by looking at the suture lines.

- **In a complete ammonite shell**, there are no suture lines for the first half whorl or so. This is where the undivided body chamber is. The suture lines only begin where the buoyancy chambers are.

- **Suture patterns** vary greatly between ammonites. All are very complicated. Some have rounded shapes, some spiky patterns and others are very wavy.

- **Ammonites** are frequently sold as ornaments. Often these are highly polished and the outer shell removed, to show the amazing suture patterns.

◀ Baculites *is an uncoiled ammonite from Cretaceous rocks. The very complex suture lines are typical of this genus.*

131

Spiny ammonites

- **Many ammonites** have sharp, spiny structures on their shells. These frequently break off during or before fossilization.

- **It has been suggested** that sharp spines on the shell helped protect the ammonite from predators.

- **A few ammonite shells** have been discovered with the impressions of jaw marks on them. These may be from a marine reptile, such as a mosasaur.

- **The spines** on ammonite shells are generally very delicate and hollow. They would probably not be much use against a predator, certainly not one the size of a mosasaur.

- **Another theory** is that spines and other structures on the outside of the shell may help with camouflage. The spines break up the shape of the ammonite shell, especially in deeper water, where light penetration is low.

- *Liparoceras* is an ammonite commonly found in rocks of Lower Jurassic age. In life, it had sharp spines on its shell. These are usually broken off in fossils, with only their stumps remaining.

- **On the shell** of *Liparoceras*, the rows of knobs where the spines were can be easily seen. There are also wide ribs running across the shell.

- **As with many ammonites**, the ribs on the shell of *Liparoceras* divide and become more numerous as they run across the back of the shell.

- **Where *Liparoceras* is found**, there is often a smaller ammonite called *Aegoceras*. This looks exactly like the inner whorls of *Liparoceras*.

- **Some palaeontologists** believe that these two ammonites are males and females of the same species.

Base of the spines

▲ *Only the*
base of the spines
remain on the shell
of this fossil Liparoceras.
The specimen comes from
early Jurassic strata.

Ammonite names

- **Fossils** are named for many reasons. Often the fossil's name is the Latin version of the name of the person who first found it.

- **Sometimes** a fossil's name is derived from the place where it was first found, or after some special feature it has. The scientific name may tell us something about the fossil's shape.

- **The Jurassic rocks** in North Yorkshire, UK can be easily observed at the coast. These strata have been studied for hundreds of years.

- **Around the town of Whitby** in North Yorkshire, the lower Jurassic rocks form high cliffs below St Hilda's Abbey. These rocks were originally layers of mud on the Jurassic seabed.

- **Many creatures** lived in this Jurassic sea. Fossils of molluscs, fish and reptiles show that the Jurassic sea was full of life.

- **The ammonite** *Hildoceras* is named after St Hilda, who founded the abbey on the cliff tops at Whitby.

- **Ammonites** are associated with Whitby to such an extent that the town's coat of arms contains three of them.

● **Famous geologists** of the 19th century learnt a lot from the strata on the Yorkshire coast. These include William Smith (1769–1839), who pioneered the use of fossils for correlating strata from one place to another.

● **Further south** on this coast, in the town of Scarborough, Smith designed the Rotunda Museum in such a way that fossils could be displayed depending on the distribution, and age of the sedimentary rock they were found in.

...FASCINATING FACT...
It was once believed that ammonites were snakes that had been turned to stone by St Hilda. Local craftsmen used to carve snakes' heads on ammonites to perpetuate the myth.

◀ *A head has been carved on this ammonite shell to illustrate the myth that ammonites are fossilized snakes.*

Giant ammonites

- **Ammonite shells** vary greatly in size. The majority are a few centimetres in diameter, some are much larger.

- **In order to study** ammonite shells and determine the average size of different species, certain rules have to be followed.

- **Before measuring** the size of a fossilized ammonite shell, it is important to make sure it is complete. This is done by examining the shell carefully and looking for the suture lines.

- **A lack of suture lines** near the shell opening shows that the body chamber is present. The shell will be complete if this is the case.

- **Palaeontologists** also have certain ways of telling if an ammonite is a small juvenile.

- **Mature shells** often have widened shell openings and the last few sutures crowd together.

- **One of the largest ammonites** is aptly named *Titanites*. It could grow to about one metre in diameter.

- *Titanites* occurs in late Jurassic rocks. It is loosely coiled and has strong ribs crossing the shell.

- **An even larger ammonite** is *Parapuzosia*, from late Cretaceous strata, which grew to 2.5 m in diameter.

- **It is probable** that such large ammonites lived near, or on, the seabed, rather than swimming freely.

▶ *This specimen of* Titanites *is just under one metre in diameter. It is on display in the Geology Department at the University of Keele, Staffordshire, UK.*

Titanites titan S.S. BUCKMAN 1921
UPPER JURASSIC PORTLANDIAN STAGE·
DORSET, ENGLAND.
"TYPE AMMONITES" VOL. III. PLATE CCXXXI
PRESENTED BY H.M. GEOLOGICAL SURVEY

Uncoiled ammonites

- **The classic** ammonite shell is coiled in a flat spiral. Some shells have a large body chamber that overlaps the smaller, inner whorls.

- **During ammonite evolution**, many different shells appeared that initially don't look like ammonites.

- **At many times** during the Jurassic and Cretaceous Periods, some ammonite species developed uncoiled shells.

- **Towards** the end of their evolution, in the late Cretaceous Period, uncoiling was common. Other strange shapes also appeared at this time.

- **One of the strangest** of these is *Didymoceras,* which occurs in the Cretaceous rocks of Colorado, USA.

- **This ammonite** is the corkscrew shape of a ram's horn, coiled in a very open spiral.

- **Many uncoiled ammonites** have a more U-shaped structure, like *Hamites,* from the Cretaceous Period.

- *Spiroceras* is from Jurassic strata. By uncoiling, it has lost the classic ammonite symmetry.

- *Spiroceras* retains some ammonite features, such as the thick ribs that run across the shell.

- **Uncoiled** ammonites were probably poorer swimmers than their coiled relatives. An uncoiled shell would not be as stable, and these ammonites may have moved slowly along the seabed, feeding.

▲ *This uncoiled* Spiroceras *shell has many ammonite features. There are ribs, and the shell tapers at one end.*

139

Ammonites as zone fossils

- **Zone fossils** help palaeontologists to put strata into sequences. They also allow strata to be linked, or correlated, from place to place.

- **For a fossil group** to be chosen for this work, it must have certain features. Ammonites are probably the best zone fossils, as they have virtually all the requirements.

- **A relative** time zone should be as short as possible. This allows very precise dating of rocks. It is not much use having a time zone tens of millions of years long. Far too many rocks form in such a huge expanse of time, and correlating them would be too difficult.

- **The ammonite** species chosen as zone fossils represent small parts of geological time.

▲ *This specimen of* Asteroceras, *is complete. Sutures are absent from the last part of the, because this is the undivided body chamber.*

- **Ammonites evolved** very rapidly into many species. Each species lived for a relatively short time before becoming extinct.

- **Because ammonites** lived in the sea and could move about, certain species are found in many different regions. They are useful in correlating strata from place to place.

- **Shells of dead ammonites** could drift on ocean currents, as modern *nautilus* shells do, and be carried to distant places.

- **A zone fossil** should be easily fossilized. A jellyfish may have all the attributes required for correlating rocks, but it is rarely found as a fossil. Ammonite shells are easily preserved.

- **It is important** for a zone fossil to be common. Field geologists need to be able to find them to do their work. Ammonites are numerous in Jurassic and Cretaceous rocks, and these periods are zoned by ammonites.

- **Because** of their varied structures, it is easy to tell one zone ammonite from another, making that part of the geological time scale easy to work out.

◀ *Dozens of* Asteroceras *species are known from many parts of the world during the Jurassic Period.* 'Asteroceras' *means* 'star horn'.

Cretaceous ammonites

- **During the Cretaceous Period**, ammonites flourished and many new shell shapes evolved.

- **Some Cretaceous ammonites** were uncoiled, with straight shells. Others were curved, and almost U-shaped.

- *Baculites*, a straight Cretaceous ammonite, is well-known for its remarkable pattern of suture lines.

- **This ammonite** is common in Cretaceous rocks in South Dakota, USA. It grew to a great size, reaching up to 2 m in length.

- *Scaphites* is a partly uncoiled ammonite from the Cretaceous Period.

- **The body chamber** of *Scaphites* is large and uncoiled. An ammonite with this structure was probably not adapted to swimming. It more likely lived on, or near the seabed, with the shell opening slightly upwards.

- *Douvilleiceras* is a Cretaceous ammonite, with the usual ammonite coiling. It had rows of large knobs running around the shell.

- **This ammonite** is widespread and common in Cretaceous rocks, and is used as a zone fossil for this period.

- *Mantelliceras* lived in the Cretaceous sea, on the bed that chalk was being deposited on. It had strong ribs running across its shell.

- **At the end** of the Cretaceous Period, ammonites became extinct. The exact reasons for this are unknown, although they had been declining in numbers of genera for some time. At the same time, many other groups of animals, both on land (for example, the dinosaurs) and in the sea (75 percent of marine plankton) died out.

▲ *This dusty, white specimen of* Douvilleiceras *is found in upper Cretaceous rocks, where chalk is the dominant rock.*

Ammonites with beaks

- **Certain ammonites** have a strange beaklike structure on the front of the shell. This is called a lappet.

- *Kosmoceras* is a small ammonite well-known for this lappet structure.

- **This ammonite** is found in rocks formed during the middle part of Jurassic time. It has ribs running across the shell and spines along the shell margin.

- **In the clay strata** where these ammonite shells occur, they are usually crushed flat, but original shell material is often preserved.

- **Much larger** forms of *Kosmoceras* are found fossilized with the smaller shells.

- **Palaeontologists** studying both these ammonites discovered that changes in their shells occurred at the same time. When a new feature developed on the small shell, the same feature appeared on the larger shell.

- **This side-by-side evolution** of two ammonites, one larger than the other, has been found to occur with other species.

Lappet

▲ *This specimen of* Kosmoceras, *with its lappet intact, is from Middle Jurassic strata.*

- **Palaeontologists** have analyzed hundreds of specimens of *Kosmoceras* in order to try and understand the evolution of the two size forms of the ammonite.

- **It is believed** that the large and small *Kosmoceras* may be males and females of the same species. This would explain their simultaneous evolutionary changes. The sexes of many modern cephalopods have a distinct size difference.

- **The exact purpose** of the lappet on the smaller fossil shell is unknown. Some palaeontologists suggest that the small shell was the male and the lappet was a display device.

Fossil squids

- **Squids are cephalopods** with an internal shell. These shells are common fossils in Mesozoic sedimentary strata.

- **The fossilized** internal shells of cephalopods are similar to squid and are called belemnites.

- **Belemnites first appear** as fossils in rocks of the Carboniferous Period, and became extinct just before or early in the Cenozoic Era.

- **The long**, bullet-shaped fossil, varying in length from less than one centimetre to 15 cm or more, is called the guard.

- **As well as the narrow**, tapering part of the shell, there is a much wider, chambered part, called the phragmocone. This fits into the wider end of the guard.

- **Belemnites** are solid objects, made of layers of calcite, so they usually retain their three-dimensional shape when fossilized.

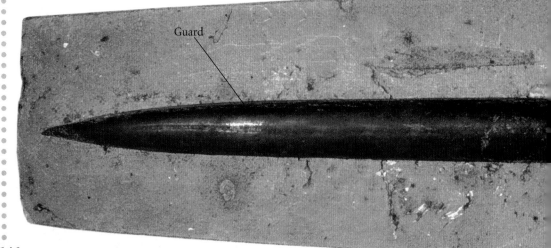

Guard

- **Where masses of belemnites occur** on rock surfaces, they are often all parallel to each other. This suggests that they were moved by seabed currents.

- **The belemnite's soft body** was like that of a typical squid, with tentacles, eyes and a funnel for squirting water or ink.

- **Belemnites** were probably free-swimming, rather like modern squids, although modern squids have not evolved directly from them.

- **Fossil** belemnite ink sacs have been found in Jurassic strata. In the 19th century, palaeontologists reconstituted the 'ink' and used it for writing.

▼ *This is an unusual belemnite fossil, as the crushed phragmocone is preserved with the narrow, tapering guard.*

Phragmocone

Tusk shells

- **Tusk shells** are alive today and are molluscs that belong to a class called the scaphopods. The earliest tusk shells occur in rocks of Ordovician age.

- **A scaphopod shell** is a thin tube that is open at each end.

- **The name** 'tusk shell' describes the way many of these shells curve and taper like an elephant's tusk.

- **Modern** tusk shells give many clues as to how prehistoric species may have lived. Today, tusk shells live in shallow seas, mainly on the continental shelf.

- **The animal burrows** at a shallow angle into the seabed sediment, and pulls itself down using a muscular foot.

- **Its head** is in the deepest part of the burrow. The narrow end of the shell, containing the anus, projects a short distance above the seabed.

- **Using specially adapted tentacles**, the tusk shell feeds on minute organisms living in the mud on the seabed.

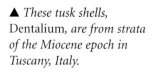

▲ *These tusk shells,* Dentalium, *are from strata of the Miocene epoch in Tuscany, Italy.*

148

- **Fossil tusk shells** are often well preserved. When the creature died, the hollow shell could easily fill with mud. This would prevent it from being crushed.

- *Dentalium* is found in rocks ranging in age from Cretaceous to Recent. It has changed little in many tens of million of years.

...FASCINATING FACT...
Fossil tusk shells have been used by people through the ages for necklaces, nose piercings and as currency for trading.

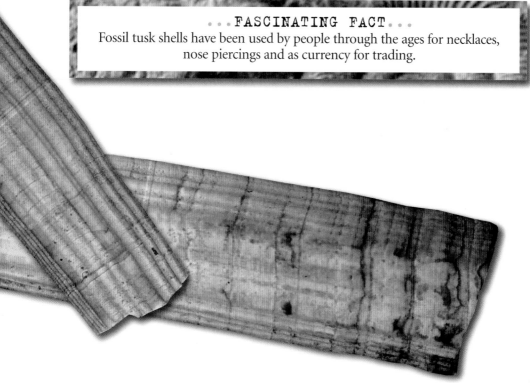

Vertebrate fossils

- **Vertebrates** are creatures that have internal skeletons usually made of bone or cartilage and incorporating a backbone. They include fish, amphibians, reptiles, birds and mammals.

- **For a number of reasons**, the fossils of vertebrates are not as common as those of shellfish, arthropods, corals and other invertebrates.

▼ Cephalaspis *was an early fossil fish from Devonian strata. Many early fish, including* Cephalaspis, *lived in freshwater lakes.*

- **Creatures** with backbones evolved much later than most invertebrates. While trilobites and brachiopods were being fossilized in the Cambrian and Ordovician periods, there were no vertebrates.

- **Many vertebrates** live on land. Here, erosion and weathering take place, rather than the deposition of sediment such as mud and sand.

- **The remains** of a vertebrate will probably decay and be broken up rather than be covered with fossilizing sediment.

- **Many vertebrate fossils** are broken and scattered bones, rather than whole skeletons.

- **There are**, however, many excellent cases of masses of vertebrates, including dinosaurs, being fossilized in deposits formed on land, such as those in China and North America.

- **Fish** were the first vertebrates to evolve. Because they live in water, many of them are fossilized.

- *Cephalaspis* was a primitive fish from the Devonian Period.

- **The large head shield** of the Cephalaspis had eye sockets on the top, and the mouth was underneath. Like the modern lamprey, it had a sucker-like mouth rather than true jaws

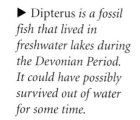

Early fossil fish

- **Vertebrate evolution** took a great step forward when fish began to survive, even for a short period of time, out of the water.

- **During the Devonian Period**, a vast continent existed comprising what is now Greenland, North America and northwest Europe.

- **The Devonian continent** was dry and mountainous, but there were great inland freshwater lakes teeming with fish.

- **The remains** of many of these fish are preserved in the muddy sandstone that formed on the lakebeds.

▶ Dipterus *is a fossil fish that lived in freshwater lakes during the Devonian Period. It could have possibly survived out of water for some time.*

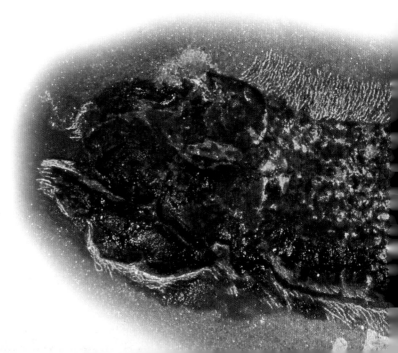

- **Fish** living in freshwater ponds and lakes are often fossilized in large numbers. If part of the lake system dries up, many fish die at the same time.

- **Fish scales** are very durable and are easily preserved as fossils.

- *Dipterus* was one of the many different fish that lived in Devonian lakes.

- *Dipterus* had a short body with a large head.

- **Its fins** had bony strengthening, which may have been able to support the weight of its body.

- *Dipterus* was very similar to modern lungfish.

Armoured fish

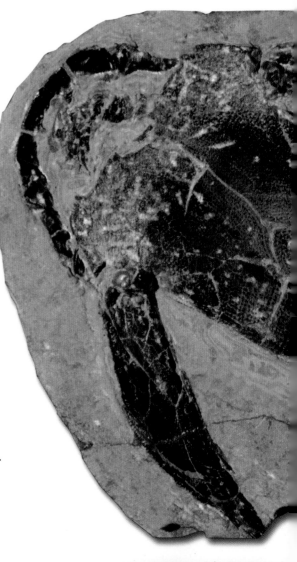

- *Bothriolepis* comes from the renowned fossil site of Miguasha near Scaumenac Bay in Canada.

- **Fossils** were first discovered at this now famous site in the mid 19th century.

- **The rocks** there contain thousands of exceptionally well-preserved fossils of fish and other organisms.

- **These remarkable** numbers of fine fossils have attracted both professional and amateur collectors.

- **In order** to prevent fossil collectors from ravaging the site, the Miguasha National Park was set up in 1985. In 1999 it became a world heritage site. Any new finds are kept in the museum there.

- **Early fish** were often covered with large scales and protective armour.

- *Bothriolepis* had a large head shield, which is the only part usually fossilized.

● **The head shield** was heavily armoured and covered with rough, bony plates.

● **Extending** from each side of the head were two long, narrow, finlike projections.

● **Palaeontologists** have cut many of the well-preserved fossils from Miguasha into sections. They discovered internal details such as two large sacs leading from the pharynx (throat). These may have been lungs.

◄ *Only the heavily armoured head shield and armlike projections of this* Bothriolepis *has been preserved.*

The Green River fish

◀ Knightia *is one of many fish species preserved in the famous Green River strata.*

- **Exceptional numbers** of fossil fish are preserved in the Green River strata of Wyoming, Colorado and Utah, USA.

- **These rocks** are limestones formed in the Eocene Epoch.

- **It seems that** during Eocene times, a number of large lakes existed in the Green River region.

- **Fossil pollen** found in the strata shows that dense vegetation grew around the lakes.

- **Many different genera** of fish lived in the Green River area. Fossils of *Knightia, Diplomystus, Gosuitichthys* and *Priscacara* are all common.

- **Small rock slabs** covered with some of these fish are sold in fossil shops.

- **The climate** in the Green River region was probably warm with definite seasons, during the Eocene Epoch.

- **In the drier season,** the lakes became smaller, and many fish died and became fossilized as the lakes dried up.

- *Gosuitichthys* is in many ways a modern fish, with its backbone near the dorsal surface and masses of ribs supporting the body.

- **Many of the Green River** fossil fish are perfectly preserved, but some are in small pieces. This may be because they exploded during decomposition.

◄ *When water in one of the Green River lakes dried up, this mass of* Gosuitichthys *died, and was covered with mud.*

157

Fossil fish teeth

▼ *This fossil tooth is from an extinct type of* Carcharodon, *which grew far larger than today's great white shark.*

● **Fish teeth** are made of very durable material, and are often the only part of the creature that becomes fossilized.

● **In some strata** formed during the Cenozoic Era, there are large numbers of fossil fish teeth, especially those of sharks.

● **Many sharks** do not have true bony skeletons, and their teeth are all that remain as fossils.

● **By comparing** fossil fish teeth with those of modern fish, it is usually possible to say what the ancient fish were like.

● **Two fossil sharks** that are known mainly from their teeth are *Lamna* and *Odontaspis*.

● **These sharks** were medium-sized predators that grew to about 4 m in length.

● **The genus *Carcharodon*** is one of the best-known fossil sharks. It also includes today's great white shark.

- **Fossil *Carcharodon*** teeth sometimes called *Carcharodon megalodon*, can be as long as 15 cm and occur in Cenozoic strata.

- **From the large size** of the teeth, it seems that this shark may have grown over 15 m in length.

- **The teeth** of *Carcharodon* are triangular in shape, with rows of sharp serrations along their edges.

▲ *The prehistoric shark Hybodus was a fierce predator, and had many rows of triangular, backward-facing teeth.*

159

Early amphibians

▼ *This fossil temnospondyl (primitive amphibian) is from Odenheim, Germany. Only an outline of its body remains, with black carbon traces of the skeleton. It resembles today's newts and salamanders*

- **The earliest fossil amphibians** are found in rocks of Devonian age.

- **The first amphibians** probably evolved from fish, such as lungfish, which are similar to *Dipterus*.

- **Modern amphibians** depend on water for survival. Most lay their eggs in water, and their young live in water before being able to breathe air and live on land.

- **Temnospondyls** are a group of early amphibians. Their fossils occur in Carboniferous and younger rocks.

- **With a bony skeleton** and limbs, temnospondyls share many features with modern amphibians.

- **Temnospondyls** had a flexible body, which was probably well-adapted to moving in damp habitats.

- **In West Lothian**, Scotland, UK, virtually complete temnospondyl skeletons have been found in rock of Carboniferous age.

- **The late** Carboniferous swamps were an ideal habitat for amphibians.

- **As well as** temnospondyl fossils, the Scottish late Carboniferous rocks contain fossils of scorpions, myriapods and spiders. These are mainly land-dwelling creatures.

- **Reptiles** evolved from amphibians during the Carboniferous Period.

Mosasaurus

▼ *Mosasaurs were excellent swimmers that hunted for fish and other prey in Mesozoic seas.*

- **During the Mesozoic Era**, reptiles developed into many different types, some living on land and others in the sea.

- **The Mesozoic sea** teemed with life, and giant sea reptiles preyed on fish, molluscs and other invertebrates.

- *Mosasaurus* was a very large marine reptile (about 15 metres long) that lived during the Cretaceous Period.

- **Often** only its sharp teeth are fossilized. These are more than 5 cm long. They curve slightly to a sharp point.

- *Mosasaurus* fossils have been found in North America and Northern Europe.

- **The body** of *Mosasaurus* was slender, and it used its powerful tail to propel itself through the water.

- **A study of *Mosasaurus* skulls** has shown that there are many similarities with those of monitor lizards, which live today.

- **Most mosasaurs** probably caught vertebrate prey, including fish. Some had teeth adapted for crushing.

- **The first *Mosasaurus*** remains were found in 1770 in the Netherlands. When first discovered, nobody knew what the giant fossil jaws were.

- **The name *Mosasaurus*** refers to the Meuse region in the Netherlands, where the remains were found.

▶ *These vertebrae and ribs of a fossil mosasaur are from Cretaceous rocks in France.*

163

Pliosaurus and Plesiosaurus

- **The fossilized** bones of *Plesiosaurus* and *Pliosaurus* are not uncommon in Mesozoic strata.

- **The lower Jurassic rocks** at Lyme Regis, Dorset, UK have been a well-known fossil site since the early 19th century. Even today, fossil collectors scour the rocks exposed on the shore.

- **The first** *Plesiosaurus* was found at Lyme Regis by Mary Anning in 1821.

- *Plesiosaurus* grew to around 12 m in length, and its most notable feature was its long neck.

- **The body** of *Plesiosaurus* was short and stout, with four large paddle-shaped limbs.

- *Plesiosaurus* had a small head, and its jaw was filled with many sharp teeth.

- *Plesiosaurus* may have fed by slinging its head at prey using its long, flexible neck.

- *Pliosaurus* was very similar to *Plesiosaurus*, but had a much shorter neck with a large head.

- *Pliosaurus* probably hunted live prey including reptiles, fish and molluscs such as ammonites.

In 1824 Mary Anning sold the first *Plesiosaurus* skeleton to the Duke of Buckingham for £100, a huge sum in those days.

◀ *This short-necked pliosaur was an active hunter in the Jurassic seas.*

Ichthyosaurus

- **Fossils** of *Ichthyosaurus* have been known since the beginning of the 19th century.

- **These fossil** marine reptiles are found in rocks of Triassic, Jurassic and Cretaceous age.

- *Ichthyosaurus* lacked the long neck of *Plesiosaurus*, and had a long, beaklike snout.

- **The mouth** was filled with conical, grooved teeth, designed for tearing prey apart.

▲ *This ichthyosaur's skeleton shows a strong spine that allowed the body to bend during movement in the water. The large eye sockets indicate good vision.*

- **The body of *Ichthyosaurus*** was streamlined, with a large, pointed dorsal fin and powerful front paddle fins. The rear pair of fins was much smaller.

- **The tail had bones** in only the lower part, and would have probably moved the animal upwards as well as forwards in the water.

- **Many remarkable** fossil ichthyosaurs have been found. Whole skeletons surrounded by a black impression of the body, including details of the paddles and tail, occur in Germany.

- **Fossils have proved** that *Ichthyosaurus* gave birth to live young. At least one adult skeleton has been found with a juvenile skeleton inside it.

- **Cephalopods**, including ammonites, had hooks on their tentacles. One *Ichthyosaurus* stomach contained the hooks from at least 1600 cephalopods.

...FASCINATING FACT...
An *Ichthyosaurus* that died giving birth has been fossilized, with the baby skeleton protruding from the birth canal.

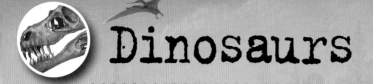

Dinosaurs

A reconstruction of a Cretaceous scene.

168

- **The dinosaurs** were a group of reptiles that evolved during the Mesozoic Era (248–65 million years ago). The name dinosaur means 'terrible lizard'.

- **All dinosaurs** lived on land. Some may have wandered into freshwater swamps but none lived in the sea.

- **Dinosaurs** are classified in a group of reptiles called the archosaurs.

- **Other archosaurs** include crocodiles and the extinct flying pterosaurs.

- **Dinosaurs** were a very varied and successful group. They lived for around 165 million years, before becoming extinct at the end of the Cretaceous Period.

- **Some dinosaurs**, such as *Diplodocus* were enormous and slow moving. Others, like *Compsognathus*, were small and nimble.

- **Many dinosaurs** laid eggs, from which their young hatched. Dinosaur nests have been found, including those of *Protoceratops* in Mongolia.

KEY

1 *Edmontonia*
2 *Stegoceras*
3 *Triceratops*
4 *Avimimus*
5 *Lambeosaurus*
6 *Struthiomimus*
7 *Albertosaurus*
8 *Corythosaurus*
9 *Parasaurolophus*
10 *Euoplocephalus*
11 *Tyrannosaurus*

- **Dinosaurs** evolved to live in many habitats and to eat different food. *Allosaurus* was a predatory carnivore (meat eater) and *Stegosaurus* was a herbivore (plant eater).

- **There are many** theories about dinosaur extinction. It is probable that a giant meteorite hit the Earth in Mexico, this would have altered the climate and destroyed food chains.

- **Perhaps dinosaurs** are not extinct. If you see a pheasant, note how similar it is to one of the long-tailed, two-legged dinosaurs. Birds are thought to have evolved from dinosaurs, and may simply be modern, feathered versions of the prehistoric reptiles.

Stegosaurus

- ***Stegosaurus*** lived during the late Jurassic Period (160–145 million years ago).

- **This was** a relatively large dinosaur, with adults growing to about 9 m in length, and possibly weighing up to 2 tonnes.

- **Fossils** of *Stegosaurus* come mainly from the western parts of North America, especially Wyoming, Utah and Colorado. Relatives of *Stegosaurus* such as *Kentrosaurus* have been found fossilized in South East Africa and fossils of *Tujiangosaurus* have been found in East Asia.

- ***Stegosaurus*** was a thick-set dinosaur that walked on all four legs.

- **Along its back**, Steg*osaurus* had a double row of large, relatively flat, bony plates.

- **The tail** of *Stegosaurus* was heavy and thick where it joined the body. It tapered rapidly to a point, and at the end it had four large bony spikes.

- **There are** a number of theories as to the function of the bony plates. They may have contained blood vessels, and so adjusted body temperature.

Brain cavity

Snout

▲ *This fossilized* Stegosaurus *skull shows the narrow snout and very small brain cavity.*

170

▼ Stegosaurus *had a tiny head in comparison to its body. Its brain was tiny too, indicating a lack of intelligence.*

- **The bony plates** could have been held flat against the body as a means of defence, and the tail spikes may have been used to swing at attackers.

- *Stegosaurus* had a very small head. The mouth had tiny serrated teeth. It is possible that food was broken down by stones in its stomach, which the animal swallowed, rather than by its teeth.

- *Stegosaurus* moved slowly, and fed on vegetation. It would probably have been preyed on by carnivores such as *Allosaurus*.

Triceratops

◀ *The horned beak of* Triceratops *was used for tearing food. The teeth, used for chewing, were well back in its cheeks.*

- ● **Triceratops** lived around 70 to 65 million years ago, during the late Cretaceous Period. It was one of the last dinosaurs.

- ● **The name *Triceratops*** means 'three-horned face'.

- ● **Most of the fossils** of *Triceratops* have been found in central North America, in Montana, North and South Dakota, and Wyoming. Fossils have also been found in Alberta and Saskatchewan in Canada.

- ● **This dinosaur** was stocky and thick-set. It grew to about 9 m in length, and weighed about 5 tonnes.

- ● *Triceratops* is easily recognized by its large frilly head shield and three large, forward-facing horns.

- ● **The shield** around the neck probably helped to control body temperature, as it was supplied with blood vessels.

- ● **The horns** may have been for defence, or to help with feeding, by pulling tree branches down towards the mouth.

- ● **With its head down** and long, sharp horns pointing forward, *Triceratops* may have been able to fight off large predators.

- ● **Walking** on all four legs, it is thought that *Triceratops* lived in herds, wandering through the Cretaceous forests.

172

Like modern male deer, male *Triceratops* may have fought
each other with their horns to secure mates.

▼ *Complete skeletons, such as this one from North America, show where the muscles and other soft tissues were attached, and allow accurate reconstructions of* Triceratops.

Compsognathus

▼ *The very delicate bone structure, teeth and skull are very well preserved in this specimen of* Compsognathus.

- **Not all dinosaurs** were large. *Compsognathus* grew to only 1.5 m in length. It probably weighed around 3 kg – about the same size as a pet cat.

- **Fossils of *Compsognathus*** have been discovered in France and Germany.

174

▼ Compsognathus *was a fierce predator of small prey such as insects, lizards and perhaps even newly hatched dinosaurs.*

- ***Compsognathus*** fossils from Germany occur in the same strata as those of the earliest bird, *Archaeopteryx*.

- ***Compsognathus*** lived during the late Jurassic Period, around 150 million years ago.

- **This dinosaur** was slender, with a very long, thin tail and a long neck.

- **The head** was large, and equipped with small, sharp teeth. The large eyes would have helped it to follow fast-moving prey.

- **With long**, thin legs, *Compsognathus* would have been able to run quickly in pursuit of prey such as lizards.

- **This dinosaur** probably fed on smaller vertebrates and on invertebrates such as worms and insects, using its two sharp claws on each hand for gripping.

- *Compsognathus* lived around warm, salty lagoons, in a richly vegetated area. Limestone that formed in the lagoons contains some of the best-preserved fossils ever discovered.

...FASCINATING FACT...
Because the fossils of *Compsognathus* and *Archaeopteryx* are so similar, palaeontologists originally mistook some *Archaeopteryx* fossils for those of *Compsognathus*.

Allosaurus

- *Allosaurus* was a fierce, predatory dinosaur that lived in late Jurassic times about 150 million years ago.

- **This dinosaur** grew to around 11 m in length, and may have weighed up to 2–3 tonnes.

- *Allosaurus* stood on its large back limbs, and used its smaller front pair for grasping prey.

- **The fingers** on the front limbs each had long, sharp, backward-pointing claws.

- **The skull** was large but lightweight. The mouth was filled with curved, serrated teeth, ideal for tearing flesh.

- **The tail** was long and tapering. This would have balanced the weight of *Allosaurus*' neck and body as it stood upright.

- *Allosaurus* fossils have mainly been found in the USA. Some fossils also occur in southern Africa and a similar type in Victoria, Australia.

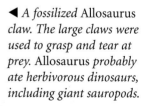

◄ *A fossilized* Allosaurus *claw. The large claws were used to grasp and tear at prey.* Allosaurus *probably ate herbivorous dinosaurs, including giant sauropods.*

▲ Allosaurus *had jaws that could bend slightly to allow them to open extremely wide. Together with its vicious front claws, this made* Allosaurus *a fearful predator.*

- **One of the most spectacular** collections of dinosaur bones ever found was a mass of over 60 *Allosaurus* skeletons. These were discovered at the Cleveland-Lloyd Dinosaur Quarry in Utah, USA.

- **It has been suggested** that these 60 *Allosaurus* had got trapped in a swamp as they attacked giant sauropods feeding there.

- **Herbivorous dinosaurs** were the main prey of *Allosaurus*. The large sauropod dinosaurs such as *Diplodocus* may have lived in herds for safety.

Iguanodon

◀ Iguanodon's 'hands' were probably very good at grasping vegetation.

- *Iguanodon* was a large, herbivorous dinosaur that lived during the early part of the Cretaceous Period (135 million years ago).

- **This dinosaur** grew to around 10 m long, and may have weighed 4 tonnes.

- *Iguanodon* walked on its strong hind legs, and may at times have also moved on all four limbs.

- **The front limbs** were designed for grasping, with long flexible 'fingers'.

- **Fossils** of *Iguanodon* have been found mainly in Europe, in Belgium, Germany and Spain. The first was discovered in Sussex, UK in the 1820s.

- *Iguanodon* was first described by Gideon Mantell, an English medical doctor and fossil collector, in 1825. His wife had earlier found the fossil teeth in a heap of stones by the road.

- **The fossil teeth** were very like those of a modern iguana. Mantell therefore named the dinosaur *Iguanodon*.

- *Iguanodon* fed on plant material, which it grasped using its hands. Its teeth, set in a beaklike snout, were for grinding vegetation.

178

On its 'hand', *Iguanodon* had a large thumb-spike. Early palaeontologists thought this was a horn that fitted on the creature's nose.

● **Over 30** complete *Iguanodon* skeletons were discovered in a coal mine in Belgium in 1878. It seems that a herd had become trapped in a ravine and had been preserved by sand and mud.

▲ Iguanodon *walked upright, using its heavy tail to balance. It may have sometimes walked on all fours.*

Saurolophus

- *Saurolophus* belongs to a group of dinosaurs classified as the hadrosaurs. They are sometimes called duck-billed dinosaurs.

- **Fossil hadrosaurs** occur mainly in North America, but some have been found in eastern Asia.

- **This group** of dinosaurs lived towards the end of the Cretaceous Period, about 80–70 million years ago.

- **Hadrosaurs** were large, upright-standing dinosaurs, which grew to around 12 m in length.

- **The hind limbs** were strong, for walking, and the front limbs much smaller, for grasping plant material.

- **Plants** were chewed by the many rows of teeth in the animal's cheeks.

- **Hadrosaurs** had unusual skulls, with wide, elongated, beaklike snouts.

- **On the top** of the skull was a bony crest, which in some genera, such as *Parasaurolophus*, extended well beyond the back of the head.

- **Many suggestions** have been made by palaeontologists for the function of the hadrosaur crest. It was linked to the nostrils by hollow passages, and may have been used for air storage, when the animal fed on underwater plants.

  - **The hadrosaur's bony crest** may have given it a very good sense of smell. This was important for a creature that was preyed on by carnivores.

◀ *The bony crest was the most distinctive feature of* Parasaurolopus. *Its exact function is not certain, but it was probably linked to the respiratory system, and may have been used to make sounds such as honks and bellows, perhaps at breeding time.*

Tyrannosaurus

- ***Tyrannosaurus*** is one of the most famous dinosaurs. Its name has become synonymous with fierce predation.

- **This dinosaur** was one of the very last to evolve. It lived towards the end of the Cretaceous Period, around 70–65 million years ago.

- **Fossils** of *Tyrannosaurus* come from Canada (Alberta and Saskatchewan) and the USA (Wyoming, Montana and Colorado).

- **The first** *Tyrannosaurus* **fossils** were discovered in 1902, and for many years only a few skeletons were known. In the last 40 years, many new finds have been made.

- ***Tyrannosaurus*** was a giant predator, growing to more than 12 m in length and weighing as much as 6.5 tonnes.

- **This huge dinosaur** stood and walked on its massive hind legs. The weight of its body was balanced by its thick tail.

▲ *There is evidence that Tyrannosaurus, and certain other dinosaurs, may have had feather-like growths on their scaly skin.*

The front limbs of *Tyrannosaurus* were
very small – no longer than our arms.

- **It is thought** that *Tyrannosaurus* could run at
  around 30 km/h, especially when chasing prey.

- **The teeth** in its huge jaws were up to 18 cm long.
  They had serrations, which would help tear flesh.

- **The skull** had very strong muscles to provide
  power to the jaws. It also had flexible areas,
  which may have helped to cushion collisions
  when attacking prey.

▼ *The skull of* Tyrannosaurus *was
flexible and lightweight. The large,
rear-facing teeth are well preserved
in this specimen.*

Deinonychus

- **Though small**, *Deinonychus* was one of the fiercest predators, equipped with vicious claws and teeth.
- ***Deinonychus*** lived during the middle of the Cretaceous Period, about 115–105 million years ago.
- **Fossils** of *Deinonychus* have been found in Montana and Wyoming, USA.
- **This dinosaur** grew to about 3 m in length and weighed 60 kg.

▶ *The skeleton of* Deinonychus *suggests that it was a fast-moving dinosaur, capable of leaping onto prey.*

- **The skeleton** of *Deinonychus* reveals that it was a very active dinosaur. It would have run rapidly, and could probably leap onto large dinosaurs as it attacked them.

- **The tail** was stiffened by bony tendons and strongly interlocking vertebrae.

- **The elongated head** contained rows of backward-facing, saw-edged teeth, and the hind feet had a large, sickle-shaped claw on the second toe.

- **Because** it was a small dinosaur, *Deinonychus* would have fed on small mammals, juvenile dinosaurs and lizards.

- **A pack of *Deinonychus*** hunting together, could have brought down a large dinosaur, jumping on it and slashing it with their claws. The stiff tail would help it balance during such movements.

- **It has been suggested** that *Deinonycthus* was warm-blooded. Birds may have evolved from this type of dinosaur.

◀ *Packs of* Deinonychus *may have been able to outrun larger dinosaurs, bring them down and kill them for food.*

Pterodactyls

- **Pterodactyls** belong to a group of flying reptiles called the pterosaurs.
- **Pterosaurs** lived during the Triassic, Jurassic and Cretaceous Periods, at the same time as the dinosaurs.
- **Pterodactyls** are found fossilized in rocks of Jurassic and Cretaceous age.
- **The first fossil** pterosaur was discovered in southern Germany in 1784.
- **At first** this fossil was thought to be of an aquatic creature. Later studies found it to be of extremely light construction, and its very long fourth finger was interpreted as a wing support.

▲ *Pterosaurs like the pterodactyls, could glide but could not fly as efficiently as most birds – their wings were far less flexible.*

- **The name** *Pterodactylus* (wing finger) was given to this German fossil.

- **The bones** of *Pterodactylus* were hollow to minimize the creature's weight – an adaptation for flight.

- *Pterodactylus* had a long beaklike snout and claws at the front corners of its leathery wings.

- **A detailed study** of the brain-cases of some pterodactyl skulls shows that these creatures had large brains, which were in some respects similar to those of birds.

- *Pterodactylus* probably flew in a gliding fashion, and may have swooped down to catch prey.

▼ Pteranodon *was one of the later and larger pterosaurs and lived about 70 million years ago. It swooped over the sea to scoop up fish. Its wingspan was up to 10 m.*

Diplodocus

▶ *Diplodocus had large eyes, but a minute, egg-sized brain.*

- ***Diplodocus*** was a giant herbivore, and it lived at the end of the Jurassic Period, around 150 million years ago.

- **Weighing** around 10–20 tonnes, *Diplodocus* was one of the lighter large quadrupeds. It was, however, the longest of this type of dinosaur, being 27 m in length.

- **Diplodocid fossils** have been found in North America, especially in Colorado and Wyoming, USA.

- **With a large body** to support, *Diplodocus* stood on four massive legs. These had hooflike claws, apart from the three inner toes, which had sharper, longer claws.

  - **The thick legs** acted like the supports on a suspension bridge, with its backbone in the same position as the roadway between them.

    - **The neck** and tail were very long. The tail tapered gradually, and had a whiplike end.

    - **A modern** interpretation of the animal's body suggests that the tail did not drag on the ground, as had been previously thought. It was almost certainly held well off the ground.

    - **The skull** of *Diplodocus* had large eye-sockets, and nostrils positioned high above the jaws, which had thin teeth set right at the front. The brain-case was tiny, about the size of a hen's egg.

  - **Like other giant sauropods**, *Diplodocus* was a herbivore. The teeth did no more than tear off leaves. In the stomach these were broken up by gastroliths (swallowed stones).

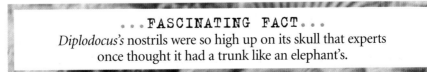

...FASCINATING FACT...
Diplodocus's nostrils were so high up on its skull that experts once thought it had a trunk like an elephant's.

189

Footprints and dinosaur movement

- **As a dinosaur moved**, it left footprints in sand or mud, just as a modern animal does. If sediment washed into the footprint impression, a trace fossil could be formed.

- **Different footprints** can be made by the same dinosaur, depending on how wet the mud is, and how fast the animal is moving.

- **As well as** individual footprints being common in certain places, there are many famous dinosaur trackways.

- **Dinosaur** trackways are found at the Paluxy River in Texas, USA, at Peace River Canyon, in Canada, and in the UK at Swanage in Dorset and near Scarborough in North Yorkshire.

- **In Queensland**, Australia, there is evidence of a dinosaur stampede, with the tracks of over 130 different dinosaurs.

- **Both the size and speed** of a dinosaur can be calculated from its footprints.

- **By studying** modern animals and their movement, a formula has been worked out that relates to an animal's length of stride, body weight and speed.

- **The trackway** at the Paluxy River in Texas shows adult sauropods moving at 3.6 km/h and smaller ones, possibly the young, walking at 4 km/h.

- **The dinosaur** stampede in Queensland, Australia, suggests dinosaurs running at 13 to 15 km/h, and a giant carnivore walking at 8 km/h.

◀ *These footprints were left by a* Tyrannosaurus. *The method of working out the animal's size, based on its footprints, can be backed up by evidence from fossil skeletons.*

...FASCINATING FACT...

Using a formula based on modern animals, it has been estimated that the fastest dinosaurs may have been able to run at speeds of 50 km/h.

191

Dinosaur eggs and nests

- **Fossils** of dinosaur eggs are not uncommon, proving that dinosaur young hatched from eggs with hard shells.

- **A hard-shelled egg** is a great evolutionary step forward from the soft eggs that amphibians and fish lay in water.

Hadrosaur egg

▶ Both these dinosaur eggs are from late Cretaceous rocks in Henan Province, China.

● **By laying** hard-shelled eggs, which were fertilized inside the mother, dinosaurs and birds no longer relied on a watery habitat.

● **Some scientists** believe that certain dinosaurs made nests of earth or mud and nested in colonies.

● **One of the earliest** discoveries of dinosaur nests was in the Gobi Desert in 1922.

● **It is difficult** to know how long a dinosaur egg took to hatch. It would depend on the surrounding temperature, and may have been many weeks.

Segnosaurus egg

● **Fossils** of *Protoceratops'* eggs show them laid in a circle, in a hollow scooped in the earth.

● *Maiasaura* was a hadrosaur (duck-billed dinosaur) found fossilized in late Cretaceous rocks in Montana, USA.

● **From fossil evidence**, it seems that *Maiasaura* lived in large herds. They may have migrated seasonally and probably bred in colonies.

● **Fossils** of *Maiasaura* nests with eggs and young have been discovered in Montana, USA.

Archaeopteryx

▼ *With a covering of feathers,* Archaeopteryx *is the earliest really birdlike creature in the fossil record.*

- **In 1861**, the fossil of an unknown creature that seemed to have the impressions of feathers was discovered at Solnhofen in southern Germany.

- **The fossils** from Solnhofen are called *Archaeopteryx*, which means 'ancient wing'.

- **This has proved** to be one of the most important fossils, as it is the earliest known bird.

- **The late Jurassic** limestone at Solnhofen is famous for its detailed preservation of very delicate organisms.

- *Archaeopteryx* has many features similar to those of small dinosaurs. Its jaws, for example, have rows of small teeth.

- **The reptilian tail** is also long and bony, and there are claws on its wing-supporting arms.

- **The presence of feathers**, and the large eyes and brain, are all true bird features.

- **The bones** in the *Archaeopteryx* skeleton are not as lightweight as those of modern birds.

- **It is probable** that *Archaeopteryx* could glide rather than fly efficiently.

▶ Archaeopteryx *feathers were proper flight feathers and were not just used for keeping warm.*

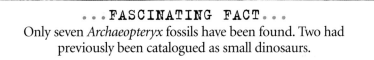

...FASCINATING FACT...
Only seven *Archaeopteryx* fossils have been found. Two had previously been catalogued as small dinosaurs.

The first mammals

- **Mammals** differ from reptiles in a number of important ways. They have fur, are warm-blooded, and feed their young with milk. Also, the great majority of mammals give birth to live young.

- **The first mammals** are found fossilized in rocks from the Triassic Period (248–206 million years ago).

- **Near Bristol, UK**, is a famous site for early mammal fossils. Here, deposits containing mammal remains from a Triassic cave floor were washed into a crack in the underlying Carboniferous limestone.

- **The early mammals** that lived at the same time as dinosaurs may have been at least partly nocturnal. Their skulls have large eye sockets, suggesting good vision.

- **In Jurassic rock** in South Africa are the remains of *Megazostrodon*, one of the best-documented early mammals.

- *Megazostrodon* had a shrewlike body and a long snout filled with sharp teeth.

- **It is thought that** *Megazostrodon* hunted at night for invertebrate prey such as insects.

- **Another early mammal** was *Morganucodon*. This rodent-like creature had very large eye sockets in its tiny skull, and may also have been nocturnal.

- **The brain-case** suggests good hearing as well as good vision. Palaeontologists studying the jaws of *Morganucodon* believe that, like some modern mammals, it may have had two sets of teeth during its life, and was possibly fed on milk when very young.

Early mammal fossils were discovered in Jurassic rocks
in Oxfordshire as long ago as 1764. Their importance
was not realized for nearly 100 years.

▼ Megazostrodon *is one of the earliest*
mammals, and its fossils have been found
in rocks of Jurassic age.

Megatherium

- **After their development** through the Mesozoic Era, many giant forms of mammals evolved in the Cenozoic.

- **Tree sloths** evolved during the Eocene Epoch (56–34 million years ago).

- *Megatherium* was a a close relation to the sloths and grew to over 6 m tall. It first appeared about 6 million years ago.

- **Fossil remains** of *Megatherium* have been found in both North and South America, mainly from cave deposits.

- **Much is known** about *Megatherium*, as it only became extinct around 12,000 years ago.

- **As well as bones**, some soft tissue and hair have been found.

- **There are stories** in Argentina that these giant sloths only died out a few hundred years ago, persecuted by humans.

- *Megatherium* had a thick tail and massive hind legs to support it when it stood upright.

- **The snout** was extended forward and it had no front teeth. The animal probably grasped tree branches with its strong front limbs and pulled off the leaves.

...FASCINATING FACT...

Large quantities of *Megatherium* dung are common in some caves in Argentina. One such deposit caught fire and burned for six months!

◄ Megatherium, *used its considerable height to feed from trees. Few other mammals could compete with this feeding strategy.*

Paraceratherium

▶ Paraceratherium, *the largest land mammal ever, had strong legs and may have been able to run quite fast.*

- **Fossilized** remains of *Paraceratherium* (formely known as either *Baluchitherium* or *Indricotherium*) have been found in Asia and Europe.

- *Paraceratherium* is classified as a perissodactyl.

- **These mammals** are characterized by having odd numbers of toes on their hoofs. Animals with hoofs are called ungulates.

- **Only about 19 or 20 species** of perissodactyls live today. Their even-toed ungulate cousins, the artiodactyls, have between 220–230 species living today.

- *Paraceratherium* lived during the Oligocene Epoch (34–23 million years ago).

- **This mammal** was a giant, hornless rhinoceros, with a long neck, and massive legs that supported its huge body.

- **The head** of *Paraceratherium* was relatively small, and, in the males, slightly dome-shaped.

- **Reaching** 5.4 m in height at its shoulder, *Paraceratherium* was the largest known land mammal ever.

- **This enormous mammal** could easily reach the tops of quite tall trees to browse on leaves.

...FASCINATING FACT...
At 20 tonnes, *Paraceratherium* weighed as much as four large elephants.
It may have lived in small groups like modern rhinoceroses.

Giant whales

▶ *The prehistoric whale Basilosaurus, which means 'king of the lizards,' was so named because the first person to examine its remains thought it was a gigantic plesiosaur – a prehistoric marine reptile.*

● **Mammals** took to the sea early during the Eocene Epoch, about 50 million years ago.

● **Most marine mammals** belong to the biological order Cetacea, which includes the whales, dolphins and porpoises.

● **One of the oldest fossil whale**, *Pakicetus,* comes from Eocene rocks in Pakistan.

● **Fossils** of the giant Eocene whale, *Basilosaurus,* were first discovered in the 1830s.

● *Basilosaurus* grew to over 20 m in length. Its body was slim, and the head, with rows of large triangular teeth, was rather small. Modern whales have large heads.

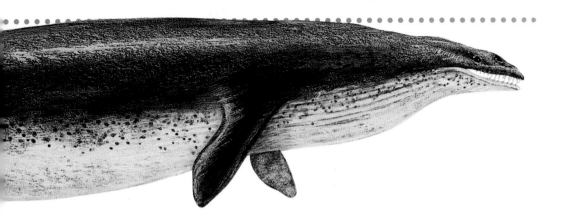

- **Instead of** a blow-hole like modern whales, *Basilosaurus* had nostrils.
- **The body** would have been able to flex in the water to provide power for swimming and the broad front flippers acted as rudders.
- **The rear limbs** were virtually non-existent. They were simply small bony structures within the body.
- **In 1990**, new fossils of *Basilosaurus* were found, which showed that the insignificant internal rear limbs had all the bones of fully formed legs.
- **The largest** known animal to have ever lived, the modern blue whale, grows to 30 m in length.

Ice Age monsters

- **The last** great Ice Age began around 2 million years ago. There have been some dramatic climate changes during this time.

- **Some mammals** grew to a great size during the Ice Age. Perhaps the best known is the woolly mammoth.

- **A fully grown** adult mammoth stood 2.8 m tall at the shoulder.

- **The mammoth's skin** was well insulated, with a thick coat of hair.

- **One function** of the mammoth's huge tusks may have been to sweep snow away from the tundra vegetation on which it fed.

- **The remains** of mammoths have been found in Europe, Asia and North America.

▲ *Woolly mammoths (1), musk ox (2) and giant elk (3) wander across the frozen tundra in search of vegetation to feed on.*

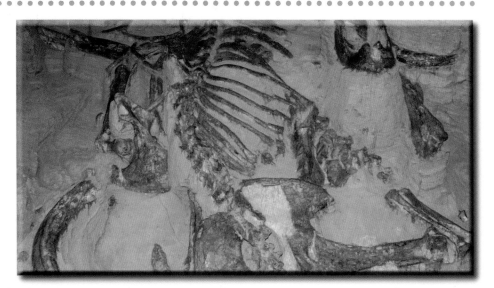

▲ *This mass of mammoth bones, including an almost complete set of ribs, is from Siberia, where it was found in frozen earth.*

- **Literally** tonnes of tusks and bones of woolly mammoths have been found.
- **Finds of mammoth tusks** have, in the past, been plundered for their ivory.
- **Our human ancestors** would have hunted mammoths for food. These elephants only became extinct about 10,000 years ago.

...FASCINATING FACT...
Mammoths fossilized in the tundra deep-freeze of Siberia
have flesh preserved well enough to be eaten.

Hominid fossils

- **Hominids** are mammals that belong to our 'human' group. These creatures are different from apes and other primates, because most probably walked upright on their hind legs.

- **There are many** different hominid fossils from various parts of the world, and it is not easy to work out a complete family tree.

- **The earliest** hominid fossils may be of a creature called *Ardipithecus* from Ethiopia.

- **An important group** of early hominids are the Australopithicenes. These upright-walking creatures lived in east and southern Africa between three and a half million and two million years ago.

- **Working in Chad**, in central Africa, a team of French palaeontologists found a hominid-like skull in 2002, which may be seven million years old. This may be a link between apes and hominids.

- **The earliest** fossils belonging to our genus, *Homo*, are the remains of *Homo habilis* from the world-famous Olduvai Gorge in Tanzania.

- **Many** other species of *Homo* have been discovered. Around two million years ago, *Homo ergaster* lived in Kenya.

- *Homo erectus* lived at the same time as *Homo ergaster* but in Europe and Asia. It became extinct only 50,000 years ago. *Homo erectus* could use fire.

- **Our own species** *Homo sapiens,* began less than 200,000 years ago in Africa. Fossils trace its spread around the world.

- **Fossils** of *Homo neanderthalensis* have been found in many parts of Europe and Asia. These hominids were highly organized, and died out around 29,000 years ago.

▶ *This skull of* Homo habilis *is flattened without a forehead. Its brain case is much smaller than ours.*

Glossary

Abyssal The deepest parts of the seabed, often thousands of miles from land.

Algae Simple, relatively primitive plants.

Calcite A common mineral composed of calcium carbonate. Calcite is found in shells and bones, and limestone is largely composed of this mineral.

Carapace exoskeleton The outer skeleton of an arthropod.

Chert A rock made almost completely of silicon dioxide. Chert often occurs as nodular masses in limestone strata. Flint is a form of chert.

Class A group of broadly similar organisms. A number of genera are grouped in a class. There are many classes within a phylum.

Compound eyes Eyes that have numerous lenses.

Continental shelf The relatively shallow part of the ocean. It extends from the shore to the continental slope, where the seabed falls to the abyssal plain.

Correlate To link strata from place to place, usually by using the fossils they contain.

Delta A deposit of sediment that accumulates where a river enters a body of non-flowing water, such as the sea or a lake.

Epoch A subdivision of geological time, shorter than a period.

Era A large part of geological time that can be divided into periods.

Genus A group of broadly similar species. Many genera make up a family, and many families make up a phylum.

Ice Age A period of time when world-wide temperatures are very low. This allows glaciers and ice sheets to develop and spread further away from the poles than today.

Igneous rocks Rocks formed when magma (molten rock below the ground) or lava (molten rock on the Earth's surface) harden into rock.

Invertebrate Creatures without an internal bony skeleton.

Metamorphism Changes that happen to existing rocks and are caused by heat or pressure, or a combination of both. Metamorphism usually occurs deep in the Earth's crust, though lava flowing on the surface can metamorphose rocks over which it flows.

Organism A living plant or animal.

Ooze Very fine-grained sediment that is found on the bed of the deepest seas.

Period A large part of geological time. Eras are sub-divided into periods.

Phylum A large group of similar organisms. A phylum is divided up into families, genera and species.

Plankton Tiny organisms that drift in the sea, often near the surface.

Quartz A very common mineral made of silicon dioxide. Sandstone is mainly made of small grains of this mineral.

Radiometric dating A way of obtaining absolute ages for rocks, based on the decay of radioactive minerals. It is mainly used for igneous and metamorphic rocks.

Reef An underwater bank of sediment or rock, the top of which is very near to sea level.

Sediment The sand, mud and other loose material from which sedimentary rocks are formed.

Species A group of virtually identical organisms that can breed with each other.

Stratigraphy The science of placing rocks in the correct time sequence.

Strip mining Mining on the Earth's surface, not underground. Any material lying above the valuable rock or mineral being mined is stripped away. This is a type of open-cast mining.

Time scale The list of eras and periods, with their dates, that are used for subdividing geological time.

Xylem Plant tissue that carries fluids and supports the plant.

Index

Entries in **bold** refer to main subject entries. Entries in *italics* refer to illustrations.

A

Aegoceras 132
Acorn worms 76
Africa,
  Allosaurus 176
  Glossopteris 38
  hominids 206
  nautilus 125
  Pre-Cambrian fossils 27
  trilobites 88
age of rocks 24
Agnostus 96
Alberta, Canada,
  Triceratops 172
  Tyrannosaurus 182
Albertosaurus 169
algae 27, **28–29**
Allosaurus 169, 171,
  176–177
amber fossils 9, *9*, 43, 85
ammonia 26
ammonites **126–129**
  ancestors 123
  beaked **144–145**
  cephalopods 120
  Cretaceous **142–143**
  extinction 17, *17*
  fossil sponges 53
  giant **136–137**
  Ichthyosaurus 167
  internal chambers *8*
  Jurassic corals 51
  molluscs 103, *103*
  names 14, **134–135**
  nodules 37
  Pliosaurus 164

ammonites (*cont.*)
  Rhynchonellid
    brachiopods 73
  rock strata 10, *10*
  spines **132–133**
  suture lines 124,
    130–131
  tusk shells 149
  uncoiled *131*, **138–139**
  zone fossil **140–141**
amphibians 150, **160–161**
  eggs 192
  nodules 37
ancestors,
  cephalopods 123
  trilobites 88, 100
animals,
  evolution 18
  naming 14
Anning, Mary 164, 165
Antarctica 38
apes 206
Archaeopteryx 175,
  194–195
archosaurs 169
Arctica 108, 109, *109*
Ardipithecus 206
Argentina 198
armoured fish **154–155**
arms,
  brittle stars 60
  crinoids 54, *54*, 58, 59
  Encrinus 56
Arthropoda 80
arthropods **80–81**
  crabs 86
  fossils 150
  insects 85
  sea scorpions 82
  Solnhofen 86
  trilobites 88, 92, 98

articulate brachiopods
  70, 72
artiodactyls 201
Asaphus 99
Asia,
  Coniopteris 42
  Ice Age mammals 204
  Palaeozoic corals 46
  Paraceratherium 201
  Saurolophus 180
  sauropods 170
Asteroceras 140, 141
atmosphere 26, 29
Australia,
  Allosaurus 176
  coal 32
  dinosaur footprints 190
  fossil algae 28, *29*
  Glossopteris 38, *39*
  nautilus 124, *125*
  Palaeozoic corals 46
  Pre-Cambrian fossils 27
australopithicenes 206
Avimimus 169

B

backbones,
  Green River fish 156
  vertebrate fossils 150
bacteria 28
Baculites 131, 142
Baltoeurypterus 83
ball-and-socket joints,
  sea urchins *62*, 64
Basilosaurus 202, 203
beaked ammonites
  144–145
bedding planes,
  carbon films 34
  graptolites 79
  Jurassic plants 43

bedding planes (*cont.*)
  Palaeozoic cephalopods
    122
  plant fossils 36
  trilobites 93
bees 98
belemnites 120, 146, *147*
Belgium,
  coal 32
  Iguanodon 178, 179
biological names 14
birds,
  Archaeopteryx 175, 194,
    194
  brains 187
  dinosaurs 169
  evolution 185
  fossils 9
  vertebrate fossils 150
birth,
  Ichthyosaurus 167
  mammals 196
biserial graptolites 78
bivalve molluscs 53, 67,
  68, 70, **104–105**, 115
  burrowing **110–111**
  Cenozoic **108–109**
  Cretaceous 149
  freshwater **112–113**
  molluscs 102
  oysters 106
Bivalvia 102
blue whale 203
blue-green algae 28, 29
body chambers,
  ammonites *8*, 126, *127*,
    129, 130, 131
  cephalopods *120*, 121
  Cretaceous ammonites
    142
  giant ammonites 136

body chambers (*cont.*)
  nautilus 124, *124*
  Palaeozoic
    cephalopods 122, 123
  suture lines 130, 131
  uncoiled ammonites
    138
  zone fossil ammonites
    140
body temperature,
  Stegosaurus 170
  Triceratops 172
bones,
  Allosaurus 177
  Archaeopteryx 195
  Compsognathus 174
  fossil collecting *13*
  fossils 8
  giant sloths 198
  Ichthyosaurus 167
  macrofossils 24
  mammoth 205, *205*
  Pleisiosaurus 164
  Pliosaurus 164
  pterodactyls 187
  vertebrate fossils 151
bony crests 181, *181*
bony plates,
  armoured fish 155
  Stegosaurus 170, 171
Bothriolepis 154, *155*
brachiopods 45, 46, 51,
    59, 63, 64, 67, **68–69**,
    90, 91,115
  fossilization 150
  living fossils 41
  Palaeozoic **70–71**
  Rhynchonellid 72, 73
  sedimentary rocks 22
brain,
  Diplodocus 188, 189

brain (*cont.*)
  hominids *207*
  mammals 196
  pterodactyls 187
  Stegosaurus 170, 171
Brazil *84*
Bristol, UK 196
Britain (*see also* UK),
  burrowing sea urchins
    67
  Jurassic crinoids 59
  Jurassic rock strata 10
  trilobites 100
British Columbia 96
British Isles 37
brittle stars **60, 61**
bryozoans 46, 64, *72*
Buckingham, Duke of 165
buoyancy chambers,
  ammonites 126, 129,
    131
  cephalopods *120*, 122,
    123
  nautilus 124
Burgess Shale 96
burial,
  coal formation 33
  fossils 8
burrowing bivalves
    110–111
burrowing molluscs 102
burrowing sea snails 116
burrowing sea urchins
    66–67
burrowing trilobites 91
burrows **20–21**
  bivalves 108, *109*
  brachiopods 68
  corals 51
  shrimp 51
  tusk shells 148

butterflies 80
butterfly stones **94–95**

C
Calamites 34
calcite (calcium
    carbonate) 8
  algae 28
  ammonites *8*
  brachiopods 72
  cephalopods 122
  corals 46, 48, 49
  crinoids 54
  oysters 107
  sedimentary rocks 22
  squids 146
  trilobites 98
Calymene 92, 93
calyx, crinoids 54, *54*, 56,
    57, *57*, 59
Cambrian Period,
  arthropods 80
  continental drift 100,
    101
  evolution 18, *18*
  fossils 150
  gastropods 115
  graptolites 76
  living fossils 41
  microfossils 24
  molluscs 102
  sponges 53
  trilobites 88, *89*, 95, 96,
    98
camouflage,
  peppered moth 19
  spiny ammonites 132
Canada,
  armoured fish 154
  dinosaur footprints
    190

Canada (*cont.*)
  Triceratops 172
  Tyrannosaurus 182
cap, crinoids 54
carapace,
  crabs 87, *87*
  trilobites 91
carbon films,
  amphibians *160*
  coal formation 34
  Ginkgo biloba 41
  Jurassic plants 43
  nodules *36, 37*
  primitive plants 31
Carbonicola 113
Carboniferous Period,
  amphibians 160, 161
  brachiopods 70, *70*, 71
  cephalopods **122–123**
  coal 32, 34, *35*
  fossil corals 45, 49
  freshwater bivalves 112,
    113, *113*
  gastropods *114*
  graptolites 76
  insects 85
  nodules 37
  sedimentary rocks 22
  squids 146
  trace fossils *20*
Carcharodon 158, *158*,
    159
caring for fossils **14–15**
carnivorous dinosaurs
    169, 190
caterpillars 85
cell structure 31
Cenoceras 124, *124*
Cenozoic Era,
  bivalves **108–109**
  fish teeth 158, 159

Index

Cenozoic Era (*cont.*)
  giant sloths 198
  plants **42–43**
  sea snails **116–117**, 118
  squids 146
centipedes 37, 80
Cephalaspis 151, *151*
cephalon 88
Cephalopoda 102, 103
cephalopods **120–121**
  beaked ammonites 144
  Carboniferous **122–123**
  Devonian **122–123**
  gastropods 115
  Ichthyosaurus 167
  molluscs 103
  nautilus 124
  squids 146
Cetacea 202
Chad, Africa 206
chalk,
  burrowing sea urchins
    66
  Cretaceous ammonites
    142, *143*
  microfossils 24
  sedimentary rocks 22,
    23
chelicerates 86
Charnia 26, 27
Charnwood Forest,
  Leicestershire, UK 27
cherts,
  fossil sponges 53
  microfossils 24
  Pre-Cambrian fossils
    27
China,
  coal 32
  crinoids 54
  dinosaur eggs *192*

China (*cont.*)
  Ginkgo biloba 41
  hominids 206
  trilobites 95
  vertebrate fossils 151
Chlamys 72
Cidaris 64, *65*
Cladophyllia 72
clams 102, 108, 110
classes of molluscs 102,
    103
classification of
  dinosaurs 169
claws,
  Allosaurus 176, *176, 177*
  Archaeopteryx 195
  Compsognathus 175
  Deinonychus 184, 185
  Diplodocus 189
  pterodactyls 187
clay,
  beaked ammonites 144
  fossil collecting 12
cleaning fossils 14
Cleveland-Lloyd
    Dinosaur Quarry,
    Utah, USA 177
cliffs 12, *23*
climate,
  dinosaurs 169
  Green River fish 156
  microfossils 24
climate change,
  extinction 16
  fossil pollen 43
  Ice Age mammals 204
clubmosses 32, 34
Clypeus 63
coal 22, **32–35**, 36
  freshwater bivalves 113
coccoliths 22, *23*, 24

coelacanth 41
coils,
  cephalopods 122
  nautilus 124, *124*
collecting fossils **12–13**
colonies,
  corals 44, 46, 49
  dinosaurs 193
  graptolites 76, *79*
Colorado, USA,
  Diplodocus 189
  Green River fish 156
  Stegosaurus 170
  Tyrannosaurus 182
  uncoiled ammonites
    139
community 53
compound eyes,
  sea scorpions 83
  trilobites 98
compression 33
Compsognathus 169,
    174–175, *195*
cone shell 118, *119*
cones 43
Coniopteris 42
conodonts 24
continental drift **38–39**
  trilobites **100–101**
continental shelf,
  Cenozoic bivalves *109*
  tusk shells 148
Conus 119
Cooksonia 30, *30*, 31
coral reefs,
  Jurassic **50–51**
  Mesozoic 50
  sedimentary rocks 22
corallites,
  corals 44, 46
  Isastrea 50, *51*

corals **44–45**, 64, 67, 71,
    73, 90, 91, 115, 116,
    119,150
  Cretaceous 149
  Palaeozoic **46–47**, 48,
    49
  sedimentary rocks 22
Corythosaurus 169
crabs 80, **86–87**
  vision 98
Cretaceous,
  ammonites 126, *131*,
    136, 139, 141,
    142–143
  Deinonychus 184
  dinosaur eggs *192*, 193
  dinosaurs *168*, 169
  extinction 16, *17*
  flowering plants 43
  gastropods 116
  Ichthyosaurus 166
  Iguanodon 178
  insects *84*
  Mosasaurus 163, *163*
  pterodactyls 186
  pterosaurs 186
  Saurolophus 180
  sea snails 118
  sea urchins 66, *66*
  sedimentary rocks 22
  Triceratops 172
  tusk shells 149
  Tyrannosaurus 182
crinoidal limestone 22, 54
crinoids 22, 45, **54–55**
  and brachiopods 73
  Jurassic **58–59**
  Muschelkalk
  limestones 56
  Palaeozoic 46
crocodiles 169

crust 8
crustaceans,
  Cambrian 96
  Cenozoic 116
Cruziana 21
crysalids 85
cuttlefish 102, 103, 120

D

Dakota, USA 142, 172
Dalmanites 91
Darwin, Charles 19, *19*
dating of rocks 10
  ammonites 140
  trilobites 88
decapoda 81
decay 34
deep seas,
  brittle stars 60
  crinoids 59
  microfossils 25
deer *204*
defence,
  Stegosaurus 171
  Triceratops 172
Deinonychus **184–185**
deltas,
  coal formation 34, *35*
  freshwater bivalves 112
Dentalium 148, 149
deposits 34
devil's toenail 107
Devonian Period,
  amphibians 160
  brittle stars 60
  cephalopods **122–123**
  corals 46
  early fish 152, *152*, 153
  insects 85
  primitive plants 30, *31*
  trilobites 92

Devonian Period (*cont.*)
  vertebrate fossils 151, *151*
diatoms *25*
Dibunophyllum 44, *45*
Dictyonema 79
Didymoceras 139
Didymograptus 76
dinosaurs **168–169**
  Allosaurus **176–177**
  Archaeopteryx 195
  bones *13*
  Compsognathus
    174–175
  Deinonychus **184–185**
  Diplodocus **188–189**
  eggs 21, *21*, **192–193**
  extinction 16, 17, 142
  footprints 20, **190–191**
  Iguanodon **178–179**
  nests **192–193**
  Saurolophus **180–181**
  Stegosaurus **170–171**
  Triceratops **172–173**
  Tyrannosaurus **182–183**
  vertebrate fossils 151
Diplodocus 169, **188–189**
  herds 177
Diplomystus 156
Dipterus 152, 153, 160
DNA,
  evolution 19
  insects 85
dolphins 202
Dorset, UK 190
Douvilleiceras 142, *143*
dragonflies 9, 85, 98
Drepanura 94, 95
duck-billed dinosaurs,
  eggs 193
  Saurolophus 180
dung 20, 198

E

Earth,
  atmosphere 26, 29
  crust 8
  extinction 16
  rock strata 10
  trace fossils 20
Echinocardium 67, *67*
Echinodermata 54
echinoderms,
  brittle stars 60
  Cretaceous 149
  Jurassic crinoids 59
echinoids 72, 73, 119
  burrowing sea urchins
    66, *67*
  sea urchins 62, *62*, 63
  spiny sea urchins 64, *65*
Ediacaran assemblage 27
Edmontonia 169
eggs,
  amphibians 160
  dinosaurs 21, *21*, 169,
    192–193
  Protoceratops 21, *21*
  trace fossils 20, 21
electricity 33
electron microscopes 24
elephants 205
Encrinus **56–57**
energy 32
England 27
environment,
  evolution 19
  extinction 16
  microfossils 24
Eocene Epoch,
  bivalves 108, 109
  giant sloths 198
  Green River fish 156
  sea snails *116*, 118, 119

Eocene Epoch (*cont.*)
  whales 202
Eparietites 130
erosion,
  ammonites *10*
  fossil collecting 12
  vertebrate fossils 151
Eryon 81, *81*
Ethiopia 206
Euoplocephalus 169
Eupecopteris 34, *37*
Europe,
  coal 32
  Coniopteris 42
  early fish 152
  freshwater bivalves
    112
  hominids 206
  Ice Age mammals 204
  Iguanodon 178
  insects 85
  Jurassic rock strata 10
  Mosasaurus 163
  Palaeozoic
    brachiopods 70
  Paraceratherium 201
  trilobites 88, 95
  eurypterids 82, 83
  even-toed mammals 201
evidence,
  evolution 18, 43
  extinction 16
  flowering plants 43
  fossils 8
evolution **18–19**
  ammonites 126, 138,
    139, 141, 144, 145
  amphibians 160
  birds 185
  bivalves 108, 112
  brachiopods 72

Index

evolution (*cont.*)
cephalopods 120, 122
corals 45
crinoids 54
dinosaurs 169, 192
early fish 152
extinction 16
flowering plants 43
gastropods 115
graptolites 78
living fossils 40
mammals 198
oxygen 29
primitive plants 30
sea snails 118
sea urchins 62, 66
squids 147
vertebrates 150, 151
exoskeleton,
arthropods 80, 81,
81
crabs 86, 87
insects 85
sea scorpions 82
trilobites 88, 91, 92, *93*,
95, 96, 99
extinction **16–17**
ammonites 141, 142
cephalopods 120
corals 44, 46
dinosaurs 169
evolution 19
giant sloths 198
Ginkgo biloba 41
graptolites 76
hominids 206
mammoths 205
molluscs *103*
sea scorpions 82
squids 146
trilobites 88

eyes,
Archaeopteryx 195
cephalopods 120, *121*
compound 83, 86
Compsognathus 175
Diplodocus 188, 189
ichthyosaurs *166*
king crabs 86
mammals 196
molluscs 103
nautilus 124, *125*
sea scorpions 83
squids 147
trilobites 88, 91, 95, 98,
99, *99*, 100
vertebrates 151

F

Favosites 46
feather star *52*
feathers 9
Archaeopteryx 194, *194*,
195
dinosaurs 169
Tyrannosaurus 182
feelers, trilobites 99
ferns 42
fertilization in dinosaurs
193
fins,
armoured fish 155
early fish 153
Ichthyosaurus 167
fire 206
fish 67, 109, 118, 119
amphibians 160
armoured **154–155**
early **152–153**
eggs 192
Green River, Wyoming
156–157

fish (*cont.*)
Jurassic seabed 134
living fossils 41
Mesozoic sea 162, 163
nodules 37
Pliosaurus 164
teeth 67, 109, 119,
158–159
vertebrate fossils 150,
151, *151*
flies 98
flight,
Archaeopteryx 195
pterodactyls *186*, 187
pterosaurs 169
flippers 203
flowering plants,
evolution 43
insects 85
flowers 43
flying reptiles 186
food chains,
dinosaurs 169
extinction 17
fool's gold *58*, *59*
foot, burrowing bivalves
111
footprints,
dinosaur **190–191**
trace fossils 20
forests,
coal 32, 34, *35*
Jurassic plants *42*
fossil record 9
Archaeopteryx 194
evolution 18
extinction 16
insects 85
fossil-bearing rocks 12
limestone rocks 22
sedimentary rocks 22

fossilization *8*
burrowing bivalves 110
Cenozoic bivalves 108,
109
Cenozoic sea snails 116
cephalopods 121
clubmosses 34
early fish 153
fish teeth 158
fossil crinoids 54
freshwater bivalves 112,
113
gastropods 115
graptolites 79
Green River fish 156
mammals 196
mammoths 205
nautilus 125
Palaeozoic cephalopods
122
Palaeozoic corals 46
Paraceratherium 201
primitive plants 31
pterodactyls 186
Rhynchonellid
brachiopods 73
sea snails 118, 119
spiny ammonites 132
trilobite vision 98
vertebrate fossils 151
zone fossil ammonites
141
fossils **89**
algae **28–29**
Allosaurus 176
ammonites *10*, *17*, 129,
130, 134
Archaeopteryx 194
armoured fish 154
bivalves 110
brittle stars 60

fossils (*cont.*)
  caring for **14–15**
  cephalopods 120
  collecting **12–13**
  Compsognathus 174, 175
  continental drift 100
  corals **44–45**, 48, 49
  crinoids **54–55**, 56
  Deinonychus 184
  dinosaur eggs 192, 193
  dinosaur footprints 190, *191*
  Diplodocus 189
  early fish 152, *152*, 153
  evolution 18
  extinction *17*
  fish teeth 158
  flowering plants 43
  gastropods **114–115**
  Glossopteris 38
  graptolites 76
  Green River fish 156
  hominids **206–207**
  Ichthyosaurus 166
  Iguanodon 178
  Jurassic ferns 42
  living **40–41**
  mammals 197, *197*
  microfossils 24
  molluscs *15*, 102, 103
  Mosasaurus 163
  naming **14–15**
  nautilus 124
  nodules 37
  oldest **26–27**
  oysters **106–107**
  plants **32–33**
  Pleisiosaurus 164
  Pliosaurus 164
  pollen 43
  Pre-Cambrian 26

fossils (*cont.*)
  primitive plants 30, 31
  pterodactyls 187
  rock strata 10
  Saurolophus 180
  sea snails 116
  sea urchins 63, 64
  sedimentary rocks 22
  sponges **52–53**
  squids 146
  Stegosaurus 170
  trace 20, 190
  Triceratops 172
  tusk shells 149
  Tyrannosaurus 182
  vertebrate **150–151**
  whales 202, 203
France,
  Cenozoic sea snails *116*
  coal 32
  Compsognathus 174
  mosasaurs *163*
freshwater creatures,
  bivalves **112–113**
  dinosaurs 169
  early fish 152, *152*, 153
  molluscs 102
  nodules 37
  vertebrate fossils *151*
frozen mammals 9
  mammoth 205, *205*
fuel, coal 22, 33
fur 196
Fyfe, Scotland *35*

G

gastroliths (stomach stones) 171, 189
Gastropoda 102

gastropods 53, 109, **114–115**
  Cenozoic sea snails 116
  Cretaceous 149
  molluscs 102
  predatory sea snails 118, 119
generic names 14
genes 43
genetics 19
genus 14
geological hammer 12
geological map 12
geological time 10
  corals 45
  day lengths 49
  graptolites **78–79**
  microfossils 24
  Palaeozoic 48
  Pre-Cambrian fossils 26
  rock strata 10
  zone fossil
  ammonites 140, 141
geologists,
  ammonite names 135
  continental drift 38
  fossil collecting 12
  nodules 37
  sedimentary rocks 22
Germany,
  amphibians *160*
  Archaeopteryx 194
  brittle stars 60
  Compsognathus 174, 175, *175*
  graptolites 79
  ichthyosaurs 167
  Iguanodon 178
  king crabs 86
  pterodactyls 186, 187
  Triassic **56–57**

Ghizou Province, China 54
giant ammonites **136–137**
giant horsetails 32, 34
giant sea scorpions 82, 83
giant sloths 198
Gigantoproductus 70
Ginkgo biloba **40–41**
glabella 92
Glossopteris **38–39**
Gobi Desert 193
goniatites,
  ammonites 126
  Palaeozoic cephalopods 122, 123, *123*
  suture lines 124
Gosuitichthys 156, *157*
graptolites **76–79**
  rock strata 10
  trilobites 96
great white shark 158, *158*
Green River, Wyoming, USA **156–157**
Greenland 152
ground sloth 198
growth bands, corals *48*, 49
Gryphaea 106, 107, *107*
guard 146, *146*

H

habitats,
  amphibians 161
  arthropods 80
  bivalves 104
  brachiopods 68, *73*
  corals 46
  crinoids 59
  dinosaurs 169

Index

habitats (*cont.*)
  evolution 19
  gastropods 115
  living fossils 40
  molluscs 102
  nodules 37
  reconstruction 48
  sea urchins 62
  sponges 52
  trilobites *90*
hadrosaurs,
  dinosaur eggs *192*, 193
  Saurolophus 180
hair,
  giant sloths 198
  Ice Age mammals 204
Halysites 46, *46*
Hamites 139
head,
  Compsognathus 175
  Deinonychus 185
  Paraceratherium 201
  trilobites 91
  whales 202
head shield,
  armoured fish 154, 155, *155*
  Triceratops 172
  trilobites 88, 91, 92, 95, 96, 99, 100
  vertebrate fossils 151
heart-shaped sea urchins 66, *66*, 67
Hemichordata 76
Henan Province, China *192*
herbivores,
  Allosaurus 176, 177
  dinosaurs 169
  Diplodocus 177, 188, 189

herbivores (*cont.*)
  Iguanodon 178, 179
  Maiasaura 193
  Triceratops 172
hexacorals 50
Hildoceras 134
  H. bifrons 14
Himalayas 10
hominids **206–207**
Homo 206
  H. erectus 206
  H. ergaster 206
  H. habilis 206, *207*
  H. sapiens neanderthalensis 206
hoofs 201
horns 172, *172*, 173
horsetails, giant 32, 34
hot springs 31
humans 19, 205, 206
Hybodus 159
Hu-die-shih 95

I

Ice Age mammals **204–205**
ichnology 20
ichthyosaurs *166*, 167
Ichthyosaurus **166–167**
igneous rocks 12
Iguanodon **178–179**
Illinois, USA 121
impression fossils 9
inarticulate brachiopods 68, 72
indicator species 46
Indonesia 124
Indricotherium 201
industrial pollution 19
insects **84–85**
  evolution 43

insects (*cont.*)
  fossils 9, *9*
  Solnhofen 86
invertebrates,
  cephalopods 120
  evolution 18
  fossils 150
  Mesozoic sea 162
  molluscs 103
Ireland 33
iron nodules 36
iron pyrite,
  graptolites 76
  Jurassic crinoids *58*, 59
ironstones 72
irregular echinoid 66
irregular sea urchins 62, 63
Isastrea 50, *51*
Italy 87
ivory 205

J

jaws,
  Allosaurus 177
  Archaeopteryx 195
  mammals 196
  Mososaurus 163
  Plesiosaurus 164
  Tyrannosaurus 183
jellyfish,
  nodules 37
  Pre-Cambrian fossils 27
  Solnhofen 86
Jurassic Period,
  Allosaurus 176
  ammonites 126, *128*, 132, *133*, 134, 136, 139, 141, 144, *144*
  Archaeopteryx 194
  arthropods *81*

Jurassic Period (*cont.*)
  bivalves 104, *105*, 110
  brachiopods 72
  brittle stars 60
  coal 32, *33*
  Compsognathus 175
  coral reefs **50–51**
  crinoids **58–59**
  Diplodocus 188
  evolution 18
  Ichthyosaurus 166
  king crabs 86
  living fossils 40, *41*
  mammals 196, 197, *197*
  nautilus **124–125**
  nodules 37
  oysters *107*
  plants 42, *42*, 43
  Plesiosaurus 164, *165*
  Pliosaurus 164, *165*
  pterodactyls 186
  pterosaurs 186
  rock strata 10
  sea urchins **62–63**, 64, *65*
  squids 147
  Stegosaurus 170
juveniles,
  giant ammonites 136
  Ichthyosaurus 167
  mammals 196

K

Kentrosaurus 170
Kenya 206
Ketophyllum 48, 49
king crabs 86
Knightia 156
Kosmoceras 144, *144*, 145

L

Lake Superior 27
lakes,
  early fish 152, *152*, 153
  freshwater bivalves 112
  Green River fish 156, *157*
  trace fossils 20
  vertebrate fossils *151*
Lambeosaurus 169
Lamna 158
Lancashire, UK 37
land,
  amphibians 161
  dinosaurs 169
  gastropods 115
  plants *31*
  molluscs 102
  reptiles 162
  vertebrate fossils 151
lappet 144, *144*, 145
larval stage, arthropods
  80
Latin names 14, 134
leaflets *36*
leaves 9
  Glossopteris 38
  nodules 36
lenses, trilobite 98
Lepidodendron 34
life 8
  evolution 18
  Pre-Cambrian fossils 27
limbs,
  Allosaurus 176
  amphibians 160
  giant sloths 198
  Iguanodon 178
  Plesiosaurus 164
  Saurolophus 180
  Tyrannosaurus 183
  whales 203

lime mud,
  Jurassic corals 50
  Palaeozoic corals 46
limestone,
  algae 29
  ammonites *10*
  brachiopods *70*, 71, 72
  cephalopods 121
  Compsognathus 175,
    175
  continental drift 100
  corals 44, 46, 49, 50, 51
  crinoids 54, 59
  Drepanura 94
  fossil collecting 12
  gastropods 115
  Germany 56
  Green River fish 156
  king crabs 86
  microfossils 24, 25
  oolitic 63
  sea urchins 63, 64
  sedimentary rocks 22
  trilobites *90*, 91, *96*,
    98
limpets 102, 115
Lingula 41, 68, *69*
Linnaeus, Carolus 14
Liocarcinus 87, *87*
Liparoceras 132, *133*
Lithostrotion 49
living fossils **40–41**
  nautilus 124
lobsters 80
  Lingula 68
  vision 98
Loganograptus 79
lungfish,
  amphibians 160
  early fish 153
lungs, fish 155

Lyme Regis, UK 164
Lytoceras 128

M

macrofossils 24
Madagascar 125
Maiasaura 193
maidenhair tree 40
mammals **196–197**
  fossils 9
  giant sloths **198–199**
  hominids **206–207**
  Ice Age **204–205**
  Paraceratherium
    200–201
  vertebrate fossils 150
  whales **202–203**
mammoths 204, *205*
Mantell, Gideon 178
Mantelliceras 142
mantle, bivalves 104
Maquokota, Illinois, USA
  121
marine animals,
  ammonites 126
  arthropods 81
  bivalves 108, 112
  brachiopods 68
  cephalopods 123
  continental drift 100
  corals 46
  extinction 17
  gastropods 115
  graptolites 76
  molluscs 103
  nodules 37
  oysters 106
  plankton 142
  reptiles 163, 166
  sea scorpions 83
  sea snails 118

marine animals *(cont.)*
  sponges 52
  trilobites 91
  whales 202
mayfly *84*
Mazon Creek, Illinois,
  USA **36–37**
Megatherium **198-199**,
  199
Megazostrodon 196,
  197
Mesolimulus 86
Mesozoic Period,
  corals 45, 50
  dinosaurs 169
  giant sloths 198
  insects 85
  molluscs *103*
  mosasaurs 162, *162*
  nautilus 124, 125
  oysters 106
  plants **42–43**
  Plesiosaurus 164
  Pliosaurus 164
  sponges 53, *53*
  squids 146
  trace fossils 21
metamorphic rocks 26
metamorphosis 85
meteorite 16, 17, 169
methane 26
Mexico 169
Micraster 66, *66*, 67
microfossils **24–25**
microscope,
  microfossils 24
  primitive plants 31
migration 193
Miguasha, Canada 154,
  155
milk 196

217

Index

millipedes 37
minerals,
  cephalopods 122
  fossils 8
  trilobites 98
Miocene Epoch *148*
Mollusca 102
molluscs 45, 46, 51, 59,
  70, 71, 73, *73*,
  102–103, 134, 162
  ammonites **126, 145**
  and corals 45, 46, 51
  and crinoids 59
  and *Pliosaurus* 164
  and sea urchins 63, 64
  and trilobites *90*, 91,
  96
  bivalves 53, 67, 68,
  104–105, 108–113
  cephalopods **120–123**,
  121
  extinction 16
  fossils *15*
  gastropods **114–115**
  nautilus **124–125**
  oysters **106–107**
  sea snails **116, 119**
  sedimentary rocks 22
  squids **146–147**
  swimming **104–105**
  trace fossils *20*, 21
  tusk shells 148
Mongolia 21, 169
monitor lizards 163
Monograptus 78, 79, *79*
Montana, USA,
  Deinonychus 184
  dinosaur eggs 193
  Triceratops 172
  Tyrannosaurus 182
Morganucodon 196

Morocco *89*
mosasaurs 132, 162, *162*,
  163, *163*
Mosasaurus **162–163**
moths 80
moulting (arthropods)
  80
  crabs 86
  sea scorpions 82
  trilobites 95
mouth,
  sea urchins 62, 64, 66
  vertebrates 151
mud,
  ammonites 134
  bivalves 108, *109*, *111*,
  113
  brachiopods 68, *71*
  brittle stars 60
  corals 46, 50
  dinosaur footprints 190
  fish 152, *157*
  fossils 9
  Iguanodon 179
  molluscs 102
  sea snails 116
  sea urchins 67
  trace fossils *20*, 21
  trilobite vision 99
  tusk shells 148
  vertebrates 151
mudstones,
  brachiopods 68
  continental drift 100
  fossil collecting 12
  graptolites 76
  Jurassic crinoids 59
  Mazon Creek, Illinois
  36
multi-celled creatures 52
Muschelkalk crinoids 56

muscles,
  bivalves 104, 105
  oysters 106
  Triceratops 173
  Tyrannosaurus 183
museums 14
musk ox *204*
mussel bands 113
mutation 19
Mya 102, 110
myriapods 161

N

naming fossils **14–15**
  ammonites **134–135**
natural selection 19
nautiloids *120*, 121
nautilus 103, **124–125**
  ammonites 126, 129, 141
  pearly 120
nectar 43, 85
nests *21*
  dinosaurs 169, **192–193**
Netherlands 163
Neuropteris 34, *36*
New Zealand 38
Newfoundland 27
newt 160
nocturnal mammals 196
nodules 36, *36*
North America,
  bivalves 112
  brachiopods 70
  coal 32
  Coniopteris 42
  continental drift 100
  corals 46
  Diplodocus 189
  fish 152
  giant sloths 198
  Ice Age mammals 204

North America (*cont.*)
  insects 85
  Mosasaurus 163
  Saurolophus 180
  Stegosaurus 170
  Triceratops 172
  trilobites 88
  vertebrate fossils 151
North Dakota, USA 172,
  173
North Yorkshire, UK 41,
  41
nostrils 203
notebook 12, 15
nummulites 25
nummulitic limestone 25

O

octopus 102, 103, 120,
  121
odd-toed mammals 201
Odenheim, Germany *160*
Odontaspis 158
Olduvai Gorge, Tanzania
  206
Olenellus *96*, 100, *101*
Oligocene Epoch 201
oolitic limestone 63
ooze 25
ophiuroids 60
Ordovician Period 91,
  150
  brachiopods 68, *69*, 72
  brittle stars 60
  cephalopods *120*
  corals 44
  crinoids 54
  sea scorpions 82
  tusk shells 148
organic limestone 22
Orkney, Scotland *31*

Orthoceras 121
Orthograptus 78
ossicles 54, 59
Oxfordshire, UK 197
oxygen 26, 27, 29
oysters 53, 102, **106–107**
ozone layer 29

P

Pacific Ocean 124, *125*
pack hunting dinosaurs 185, *185*
Pakicetus 202, *202*
Pakistan 202
Palaeocene Epoch 108
palaeontologists,
    ammonites 132, 136, 140, 144, 145
    armoured fish 155
    brachiopods 68
    Compsognathus 175
    fossils 9
    hominids 206
    Iguanodon 179
    mammals 196
    rock strata 10
    Saurolophus 181
    squids 147
    trilobites 88, 96
palaeontology 9, 14
Palaeozoic Era,
    brachiopods **70–71**
    cephalopods 121, 122
    corals 44, **46–47**
    gastropods 115
    graptolites 78
    primitive plants 30
    sea scorpions 82
    time recording **48–49**
    trace fossils 21
pallial line 110

Paluxy River, Texas, USA 190
palynology 24
Paraceratherium **200–201**
Paradoxides 88, *89*
Parapuzosia 136
Parasaurolophus 169, 181, *181*
Parka 30
Peace River Canyon, Canada 190
pearly nautilus 103, 120, 124, *125*
peat 33, 34
Pecten 102, 104, 105
pectens 53
pedicle, brachiopods 68, 72
pencil urchin *62*
Pentacrinus 58, 59
peppered moth 19
perissodactyl 201
Permian Period 88
    coal 32
    corals 44, 45
    gastropods 115
    Ginkgo biloba 41
    sea scorpions 82
Pholadomya 110
photosynthesis 32
phragmocone 146, *147*
Phyllograptus 79
phylum,
    arthropods 80
    brachiopods 68
    crinoids 56
    graptolites 76
    molluscs 102
pine trees 43, 85
plankton,
    extinction 17, 142

plankton (*cont.*)
    feeders 60
    gastropods 115
    graptolites 78, 79
    microfossils 24, 25
plant cells 27
plants,
    Cenozoic **42–43**
    coal **32–35**
    evolution 18
    extinction 17
    fossils 8, 9, **32–33**
    genes 43
    Glossopteris 38
    macrofossils 24
    Mesozoic **42–43**
    naming 14
    nodule fossils 36, 37
    primitive **30–31**
    sedimentary rocks 22
    stems 8
plaster *13*
plate tectonics 38, 39
plates, sea urchins 62, 63, 66
Plesiosaurus **164–165**
Pleistocene Epoch 87, *87*
Pliocene Epoch *109*
pliosaur *165*
Pliosaurus **164–165**
Poland 79
Poleumita 115
pollen,
    evolution 43
    Green River fish 156
    insects 85
    microfossils 24
pollution 19
polyp 44
porpoises 202

pound stones 63
Pre-Cambrian Era,
    algae 29
    evolution 18
    fossils 26, *26*, 27
    trilobites 88
predatory sea snails **118–119**
primates 206
primitive life 26
    animals 18
    evolution 18
    plants **30–31**
Priscacara 156
Productus 70, 71, *71*
Protoceratops 169
    eggs 21, *21*, 193
Psammechinus 64, 65
Pseudopecten 104
Psiloceras 126, *127*
Pterobranchs 76
pterodactyls **186–187**
Pterodactylus 187
pterosaurs 169
    pterodactyls 186, *186*
Pterygotus 82
pygidium 9

Q

quartz 8
Queensland, Australia 190

R

Radiolaria 24
radiometric dating 10
radula 119, *119*
Raphidonema 53, *53*
razor shells 110, *111*

Index

reefs 73, *90, 91, 115*
  coral 45, 46, 49, **50–51**
  sedimentary rocks 22
regular echinoids 62, 64
relative dating of rocks
  10
  using ammonites 140
  using bivalves 113
removing fossils *13*
reptiles 196
  Archaeopteryx 195
  Carboniferous age 161
  dinosaurs 169
  Ichthyosaurus 166
  Jurassic seabed 134
  mosasaurs 162
  Pliosaurus 164
  pterodactyls 186
  vertebrate fossils 150,
   151
resin 43, 85
Rhabdophyllia 72
rhinoceros 201
Rhynchonellid
  brachiopods **72–73**
Rhynie chert 31
rivers,
  freshwater bivalves 112,
   113
  trace fossils 20
rock dating 10
  ammonites 140
  bivalves 113
rock strata 10, 12, 20
  ammonites 135, 140,
   144
  bivalves 108, 109, 110,
   113
  brachiopods *69*
  brittle stars 60
  Compsognathus 175

rock strata (*cont.*)
  crinoids 59
  extinction 16
  fish teeth 158
  gastropods 115
  graptolites 78
  Green River fish 156
  molluscs *103*
  sea urchins 64
  squids 146
  trace fossils 21
  zone fossils 140
rocks,
  fossil collecting 12
  fossils 9
  Pre-Cambrian fossils
   26
  record of evolution 18
  record of extinction 16
  removing 14
  trace fossils 20
rocky coasts 12
roots,
  crinoids 54
  plants 30, 34
Rotunda Museum,
  Scarborough, UK 135
rugose corals 44, 45, 46
Russia,
  Pre-Cambrian fossils
   27
  Fossil plants and coal
   33
  hominids 206

S

salamander 160
salt water 102
sand,
  bivalves 108, *109, 111*
  brachiopods 68

sand (*cont.*)
  brittle stars 60
  coal formation 34
  dinosaur footprints
   190
  fossils 9
  Iguanodon 179
  molluscs 102
  sea urchins 67
  trace fossils 21
  vertebrate fossils 151
sand dollars 63
sandstone,
  crabs 87, *87*
  early fish 152
  fossil collecting 12
  Rhynchonellid
   brachiopods 72
  strata *35*
Saskatchewan, Canada
  Triceratops 172
  Tyrannosaurus 182
Saurolophus **180–181**
sauropods 170
  Allosaurus predation
   176, 177
  footprints 190
scales, fish 153, 154
scallops 102, *104, 105*
Scandinavia 27
Scaphites 142
scaphopods 148
Scarborough, UK,
  ammonites 135
  dinosaur footprints
   190
Scaumenac Bay, Canada
  154
scientific names 14, 20,
  134
Scleractinian corals 50

scorpions 86
  arthropods 80
  Carboniferous age 161
  giant sea **82–83**
  Mazon Creek 37
Scotland,
  amphibians 161
  brittle stars 60
  coal 32, *35*
  continental drift 100
  primitive plants 31
sea level change 16
sea lilies 54
sea organisms,
  ammonites 141
  cephalopods 120
  fossils 9
  reptiles 162
sea pen *26*, 27
sea scorpions, giant
  82–83
sea snails 115, **116–119**
sea urchins,
  burrowing **66–67**
  evolution 18
  fossil crinoids 54
  Jurassic **62–63**
  Muschelkalk crinoids
   57
  predatory sea snails 118
  sedimentary rocks 22
  spiny **64–65**
seabed 134
  ammonites 136, 139,
   142
  bivalves 108, 110, *111*
  brachiopods 68, *71, 73*
  crinoids 59
  fossil collecting 12
  gastropods *114,* 115
  microfossils 25

seabed (*cont.*)
oysters 106, 107
sea snails 116
sea urchins 66
sponges 53
trace fossils 20, *20*
trilobite 99
tusk shells 148
seawater microfossils 24
sediment,
bivalves 108
brittle stars 60
clubmoses 34
coal formation 33
fossils 8, 9, 151
rock strata 10
sea urchins 66
sponges 53
sedimentary rocks,
ammonites 135
fossils 12, 22
microfossils 24
molluscs 103
squids 146
trace fossils 20
trilobites 93
seed ferns,
coal formation 34
Glossopteris 38
nodules *36, 37*
Segnosaurus 192
senses 181
septa 126
shales *35*
brachiopods 68
crinoids 59
graptolites 76
nodules 36
shallow seas,
bivalves 108
brachiopods 70

shallow seas (*cont.*)
brittle stars 60
continental drift 100
crinoids 59
gastropods 115
oysters 106
sea snails 116
sea urchins 65, 67
trilobites 91
tusk shells 148
sharks 158
shellfish,
bivalves 105
brachiopods 68
fossils 150
living fossils 41
oysters 106
shells,
ammonites 8, 126, 129,
130, 131, 132, *133*,
136, 138, 141, 142,
144
bivalves 104, *104*, 105,
108, 110, *111*, 112,
113
brachiopods 68, *69*, 70,
71, 72
cephalopods 120, *120*,
121, 122, 123
corals 50, 51
dinosaur eggs 192, 193
fossils 8, 9
gastropods 115
macrofossils 24
molluscs 102
nautilus 124, *124*, 125
oysters *106*
sea snails 116, *116*, 119
sea urchins 62, *62*, 64
sedimentary rocks 22,
23

shells (*cont.*)
squids 146
tusk **148–149**
shelly limestone 22, 23, 56
shrimps 80
burrows 51
Solnhofen 86
trace fossils 21
Siberia,
coal 32
mammoths 205, *205*
silica 27
microfossils 24
primitive plants 31
sponges 53
silt,
coal formation 34
sea snails 116
Silurian Period,
brittle stars 60
corals 45, 46, *48*, 49
graptolites 78
primitive plants 30
sea scorpions *83*
trilobites **90–91**, 92
single-celled organisms
24, 25
Siphonia 53
siphons 110
siphuncle 124, 126
skeletons,
Allosaurus 177
amphibians 160, *160*,
161
Archaeopteryx 195, *195*
Deinonychus 184, 185
dinosaur footprints *191*
ichthyosaurs *166*, 167
Iguanodon 179
Pleisiosaurus 165
sharks 158

skeletons (*cont.*)
Triceratops 173
Tyrannosaurus 182
vertebrate fossils 150, 151
skin 204
skull,
Allosaurus 176
Compsognathus 174
Diplodocus 189
hominids 206, *207*
mammals 196
Mosasaurus 163
pterodactyls 187
Saurolophus 180, 181
Stegosaurus 170
Tyrannosaurus 183,
183
sloths, giant **198–199**
slugs 102, 115
Smith, William 135
snails,
gastropods 115
molluscs 102
sea **116–117**, 118
soft-bodied creatures
26
evolution *18*
Solen 110
Solnhofen limestone,
Archaeopteryx 194
Compsognathus 175
king crabs 86
South Africa,
living fossils 41
mammals 196
sauropods 170
South America,
giant sloths 198
Glossopteris 38
Jurassic rock strata 10
trilobites 88

Index

South Dakota, USA,
  ammonites 142
  Triceratops 172
Spain 178
species 10
  extinction 16
  naming 14
  zone fossils 141
specific names 14
Sphenopteris 34
spicules 53
spiders 37, 80, 161
spines,
  ammonites 129,
    132–133, 144
  brachiopods 71, *71*
  sea urchins 62, *62, 63*,
    64–65, 67
  trilobites 88, 95, 100
Spirifer 70, *70*, 71
Spiroceras 139, *139*
sponges **52–53**, 67
spores 30
squids 102, 103, 120,
  146–147
starfish 22
  brittlestars 60
  fossil crinoids 54
  Muschelkalk crinoids
    57
starfish beds 60
Star horn 141
Stegoceras 169
Stegosaurus 169, **170–**
  171
stems,
  crinoids 59
  plants 30, *30, 31*, 34, 54,
    54
Stigmaria 34
stipe 76, *77, 78, 79*

stomach stones
  (gastroliths),
  Diplodocus 189
  Stegosaurus 171
straight ammonites
  142
straight-shelled
  nautiloids *120*, 121
Straparollus 114, 115
streams,
  fossil collecting 12
  freshwater bivalves 112,
    113
stromatolites 28, 29, *29*
Struthiomimus 169
Sussex, UK 178
suture lines,
  ammonites *10*, 126,
    127, **130–131**, 136,
    140, 142
  cephalopods 123, *123*
  nautilus 124
swamp forests *33, 42*
swamps,
  Allosaurus 177
  amphibians 161
  coal 32, *33*
  dinosaurs 169
  freshwater bivalves
    113
  insects 85
Swanage, Dorset, UK
  190
Sweden 96
swimming,
  ammonites 129, 136,
    139, 142
  molluscs 102, **104–105**
  mosasaurs *162*
  squids 147
  whales 203

T
tabulate corals 44, 45,
  46
tails,
  Allosaurus 176
  Archaeopteryx 195
  Compsognathus 175
  Deinonychus 185
  Diplodocus 189
  giant sloths 198
  Ichthyosaurus 167
  Stegosaurus 170, 171
  trilobites 91, 92
  Tyrannosaurus 182
Tanzania 206
teeth,
  Allosaurus 176
  Archaeopteryx 195
  Compsognathus 174,
    175
  Deinonychus 184, 185
  fish **158–159**
  giant sloths 198
  Ichthyosaurus 166
  Iguanodon 178
  macrofossils 24
  mammals 196
  Mosasaurus 163
  Pleisiosaurus 164
  Saurolophus 180
  Stegosaurus 171
  Triceratops 172
  Tyrannosaurus 183,
    183
  whales 202
temnospondyls 160, *160*,
  161
terebratulid brachiopods
  74–75
test 62, *62*
Texas, USA 190

The Origin of Species 19
The Origins of the
  Continents 38
thecae 76, *77*, 78
Thecosmilia 72
theory of evolution *19*
thorax, trilobites 91, 92,
  95, 96
time recording 10,
  48–49, 78
Titanites 136, *136*
tower screw shells 116
towershells 116
trace fossils **20–21**
  dinosaur footprints
    190
tracks **20–21**
  dinosaur footprints
    190
trails **20–21**
  trilobite 93
Traumatocrinus 54, *54*
tree sloths 198
Triassic Period,
  coal 32
  crinoids 54
  Germany **56–57**
  Ichthyosaurus 166
  mammals 196
  microfossils 24
  pterosaurs 186
Triceratops 169, **172–173**
trilobites 45, 46, 71, 81
  88–89, 95, **96–97**
  arthropods 81
  continental drift
    100–101
  defence **92–93**
  evolution 18, *18*
  fossilization 150
  king crabs 86

trilobites (*cont.*)
  sedimentary rocks 22
  Silurian **90–91**
  trace fossils 21
  vision **98–99**
Trimerus 90, 91
Trochid *72*
tube feet 62
Tuojiangosaurus 171
tundra *204*
  mammoths 205
Turritella 116, *116*
turretshells 116
Tuscany, Italy *148*
tusk shells 102, **148–149**
tusks, mammoth 204,
  205
Tyrannosaurus 169,
  182–183, *191*

U

UK,
  ammonites *127*, 134
  amphibians 161
  coal 32
  dinosaur footprints
  190
  Ginkgo biloba 41, *41*
  Iguanodon 178
  mammals 196, 197
  Palaeozoic corals 46
  Plesiosaurus 164
Ukraine *83*
ultra-violet radiation 29
umbo, bivalves 104, 105,
  110
uncoiled ammonites *131*,
  138–139, 142
ungulates 201
uniserial graptolites 78
universities 14

USA,
  Allosaurus 176, 177
  cephalopods 121
  coal 32
  Cretaceous ammonites
  142
  Deinonychus 184
  dinosaur eggs 193
  dinosaur footprints
  190
  Diplodocus 189
  Green River fish 156
  Pre-Cambrian fossils 27
  Stegosaurus 170
  trilobites 93
  Tyrannosaurus 182
  uncoiled ammonites 139
Utah, USA,
  Allosaurus 177
  Green River fish 156
  Stegosaurus 170

V

valves,
  brachiopods 68, 70,
  72
  burrowing bivalves 110
  molluscs 102
  oysters 106, 107
  swimming bivalves 104,
  104, 105, *105*
vascular plants 30
vase sponge *52*, *53*
Vastergotland, Sweden
  96
veined plants 30
Venericardia 108
venom 119, *119*
vertebrate fossils **150–151**
  early fish 152
Victoria, Australia 176

vision,
  ichthyosaurs *166*
  mammals 196
  trilobites **98–99**

W

Wales 100
warm-blooded animals,
  Deinonychus 185
  mammals 196
wasps 98
water depth 46
water vapour 26
weathering 151
Wegener, Alfred 38
West Lothian, Scotland
  161
Western Australia 28
whales **202–203**
whelk *119*
Whitby, UK 134
whorls,
  ammonites 126, *127*,
  130, 131, 132, 138,
  140
  cephalopods 122
  nautilus 124
  sea snails 116
Williamsonia 42, 43
wings,
  Archaeopteryx 195
  dragonflies 9
  insects *84*
  pterodactyls 186, *186*,
  187
woolly mammoths 204,
  204
worms,
  nodules 37
  Pre-Cambrian fossils 27
  sea snail predation 118

worms (*cont.*)
  Solnhofen limestone
  86
wrapping specimens 12
Wyoming, USA,
  Deinonychus 184
  Diplodocus 189
  Green River fish 156
  Stegosaurus 170
  Triceratops 172
  Tyrannosaurus 182

X

xylem cells 30

Y

Yorkshire, UK,
  ammonites *127*, 134,
  135
  dinosaur footprints 190
  Ginkgo biloba 41, *41*
young,
  dinosaurs 190, 192
  Ichthyosaurus 167
  Maiasaura 193
  mammals 196
  Protoceratops 21

Z

zone fossils 10
  ammonites 126,
  140–141, 142
  cephalopods 123
  corals 45
  graptolites 78
  nautilus 125
  trilobites 88
zooids 76

Acknowledgements

The publishers would like to thank the following
artist whose work appears in this book:

Mike Saunders

All other artworks are from the Miles Kelly Artwork Bank

The publishers would like to thank the following picture
sources whose photographs appear in this book:

Page 22 Michael Siller/Fotolia.com
Page 121 Christian13/Fotolia.com
Page 125 Bradford Lumley/Fotolia.com
Page 173 Louie Psihoyos/CORBIS
Page 166 Johnathon Blair/CORBIS

All other photographs courtesy of
Chris and Helen Pellant